SHORT SEA SHIPPING 1995

—— by ——

Gilbert Mayes

and

Bernard McCall

INTRODUCTION

It was in the mid-1950s that, as a young schoolboy, I first became aware of the "ABC" series of books publishe by that notable transport publishing house of Ian Allan. At first, it was the inevitable trainspotting books but have a vivid memory of seeing and buying *ABC Ocean Freighters* at the bookstall on Lytham (Lytham ! Annes) station in 1957. At last I could find out more about the ships I used to see on my occasional visits ! Preston dock - and underline their names too! I soon discovered that most of the ships were too small t feature in that book so the search began for *ABC Coastal Ships* .

During the next twenty years, Ian Allan tried various formats for its shipping titles and it is significant that i! final "ABC" of coasters was published in 1975 and was compiled by my co-author Gil Mayes. That volum included tugs and trawlers along with conventional coasters. Since that time, a couple of small publishers hav produced pocket reference books in the Ian Allan style but nothing new has appeared since 1988. There ca be little doubt that the demand for such a book exists, a demand among the professionals in the shippin industry and among enthusiasts.

This present volume hopefully meets the needs of both professionals and enthusiasts. It aims to provide a immediate source of information about the ships themselves and about their operators. It also aims to presen the information in an attractive way. For this reason, we feel that the A5 size permits better photographi presentation and is preferable to the "pocket book" style.

British coastal shipping has changed almost beyond recognition since the mid-1950s. The traditiona concept of a "shipowner", be it an individual or a family, has virtually disappeared and it can now be ver difficult to discover exactly who is the benificial owner of any individual ship. This has been reflected in th book. It is often more convenient to use the word "operator" rather than owner and even that can pos problems. We admit to inconsistency in using terms such as "agents for" and "managers for"; what we hav done is to follow the wishes of the operators themselves and label their operations in the ways which they hav requested. We are grateful to all the operators listed for their assistance and support in compiling this book We have endeavoured to check all details with the utmost thoroughness, but we would be grateful to b informed of any errors which may have appeared. We cannot however accept any responsibilities for errors o. omissions or their consequences.

Readers will soon see for themselves the complexities of coastal shipping operations. This book include examples of overseas companies using "British" flags for their ships, while British and Irish Republi companies use foreign flags. There is even debate over what exactly is the "British" flag - does it for instance include the Isle of Man flag?

Equally complex is the question of ship dimensions and this book is being published at a time when th "gross tonnage" concept is changing and ships are being remeasured. We do not intend to explore this question further here; all that we can say is that the quoted measurements are the latest available at the time o going to press. Ship details are corrected to 31st December, 1994.

For each ship, the information given is as follows:

	Col 1	Col 2	Col 3	Col 4	Col 5	Col 6	Col 7	Col 8
SHIP NAME	Year	Gross	Deadwt	Length	Breadth	Draught	Service	Ship
(followed in brackets by	Built	Tonnage	Tonnage	(LOA)	Extreme	Loaded	Speed	Type
previous names and year								
of name change)								

We hope that this book will be updated regularly, perhaps every two years. We also hope that users will let us have their views on the usefulness of the book and its contents. There are many to whom we owe a debt of thanks - to the many operators who have provided information, encouragement and support; to *Lloyd's Register of Shipping* ; to those who have provided photographs; and to lots of individuals who have given an important snippet of information or answered a small query. We also thank our families for their ongoing patience and support.

Gil Mayes   Bernard McCall
(Launcherley)   *(Portishead)*

ACOMARIT (U.K.) LTD.

8 Rutland Square, Edinburgh, EH1 2BU (0131 221 9441/fax 0131 221 9313)

Technical Managers for:
Liquid Gas Shipping Ltd

ARQUIN GLEN	91	2985	4500	88,4	14,2	5,1	15		lpg
ARQUIN GROVE	92	2985	3590	88,3	14,2	6,2	14		lpg
ARQUIN MARINER	92	3693	4400	99,4	15,0	6,4	14		lpg

Pentland Gas Carriers Ltd

ARQUIN RANGER	94	4317	5771	105,4	15,7	7,0	15		lpg

Tarquin Shipping Co S.A.

ARQUIN TRADER	88	3595	4320	98,3	15,0	6,6	15		lpg

Tarquiniul Compagnia di Navigazione

ARQUIN ROVER *(r)*	94	5800	6800	105,1	16,8	9,0	15		lpg

(Launched as Val Metavro)

TARQUIN NAVIGATOR *(r)* Spring 95		5800	6800	105,1	16,8	9,0	15		lpg

Note. Flag - all Liberia except *(r)* - Italy

ADOHR ISLAND TRADING LTD.

Kilronan, Aran Islands, Co. Galway, Irish Rep.

NEWFYNE	65	199	253	33,3	7,3	2,7	9		gen

(ex Glenfyne-88)

AGRI-TRANS LTD.

4 Jocelyn Court, Dundalk, Co Louth, Irish Rep. (42 39320/fax 42 26623)

Managers for:
Onesimus Dorey (Shipowners) Ltd demise chartered to **Dundalk Shipowners Ltd**, Dundalk

SEA BOYNE *	77	999	2196	79,1	12,4	4,8	12		gen(104c)

(ex Rockabill-93, Sybille-91, Echo Carrier-89, Scot Venture-88, Sybille-88)
See also DUNDALK SHIPOWNERS * Time chartered to SEACON LTD *qv*

C. F. AHRENKIEL SHIPMANAGEMENT (CYPRUS) LTD.

Omiros & Araouzos Tower, 25 Olympion Street, PO Box 3594, Limassol, Cyprus (05 359731/fax 05 359714)

Managers for:
C. F. Ahrenkiel (IoM) Ltd

MB AVON	92	2373	4220	88,3	13,2	5,5	12		gen(96c)
MB CLYDE	92	2373	4245	88,3	13,2	5,5	12		gen(96c)
MB HUMBER	91	2373	4250	88,3	13,2	5,5	12		gen(96c)
MB THAMES	92	2373	4250	88,3	13,2	5,5	12		gen(96c)

Note. All Liberia flag

ALEXANDERS PARTNERS (SHIPBROKING) LTD.

267 Cranbrook Road, Ilford, Essex, IG1 4TG (0181 518 3190/fax 0181 518 3009)

Chartering Managers/Agents for:
Aniara Maritime Ltd

ROMEO *(c)*	83	1908	3165	81,6	14,1	5,4	11		gen

(ex Andromeda-93)
Roca Shipping Ltd

KISH *(b)*	78	1961	2973	84,2	14,0	5,4	14		gen

(ex Niewiadow-93, Launched as Ran)

Roma Maritime Ltd

ELSBORG *(c)*	77	1598	3150	81,0	13,9	5,4	12	ge▪

(ex Artemis-94, Elsborg-88, Carebeka IX-83)

Ronel Shipping Ltd

CERTAIN *(c)*	77	932	1560	65,7	10,8	4,3	11	ge▪

(ex Concert Trader-94, Flevo-92. Plato-88, Flevo-81)

The Sun Shipping Corp

BELGRAVE *(b)*	78	1059	1559	66,9	10,8	4,1	11	gen(58c)

Note. Flag - (b) - Bahamas (c) - Cyprus

ALDERNEY SHIPPING CO LTD.

White Rock, St Peter Port, Guernsey, CI, GY1 2LN (01481 724810/fax 01481 724810) and

11 Victoria Street, Alderney, via Guernsey, CI (01481 822828/fax 01481 822065)

Agents only for:

Felix Shipping Ltd

ISIS *(o)*	78	664	953	57,5	10,1	3,4	11	ger

(ex Deer Sound-94, David Dorman-89)

Allied Coasters Ltd

Chartered tonnage:

Reederei Jurgen Ohle KG m.s. "Jana"

JANA *(s)*	66	1069	1220	68,4	10,6	3,9	12	gen(44c)

(ex Jan Suhr-81, Siegerland-74)

Note. Flag - (o) - IoM (s) - Germany

ALLANTONE SUPPLIES LTD.

139 Hamilton Road, Felixstowe, Suffolk, IP11 7BL (01394 670001)

ONWARD MARINER	70	239	339	40,2	6,7	2,5	8	tk▪

Managers for:

3i PLC

CONVEYOR	80	198	307	33,5	6,6	2,4	7	tk▪

ALPHA TRANSPORTS S.A.

224 boulevard Saint-Germain, 75007, Paris, France.

Managers for:

Shamrock Shipping

CATTLE TRAIL

ONE *(m)*	70	1966	3600	100,4	14,4	6,2	14	l/s

(ex Sahara-94, Cavallino-75)

CATTLE TRAIL

TWO *(j)*	68	3342	3485	100,0	14,6	6,2	14	l/s

(ex Samir One-94, Samir 1-93, Taibah V-92, Afros-85, Bore V-77)

Note. Flag - (j) - St Vincent & the Grenadines (m) - Malta

AMBRA SHIPMANAGEMENT LTD.

3 Archbishop Makarios III Avenue, P O Box 6668, Limassol, Cyprus (05 350469/ fax 05 352937)

Managers for:

Westermoor Shipping Co Ltd

WEST MOOR	77	3807	4150	97,5	16,0	5,7	14	gen(284c)

(ex Westermoor-86, Essex Courage-83, Westermoor-83)

Note. Bermuda flag

ANGLO DUTCH MANAGEMENT SERVICES LTD.

'O Box 1, Woking, Surrey, GU22 0YL (01483 757563/fax 01483 757593)

Managers for:
Cotrasa Trading Ltd

COTFIELD *(c)*	74	1545	2946	83,5	14,1	5,1	12	gen

(ex Mechaela-93, Virgo-92, Fairmead-86, Hyde Park-82, Syon Park-74)

Streamforce Ltd

ENFIELD *(j)*	74	526	770	53,5	9,8	3,2	9	gen

(ex Glencloy-94)

Note. Flag - (c) - Cyprus (j) - St Vincent & the Grenadines

ARKLOW SHIPPING LTD.

North Quay, Arklow, Co.Wicklow, Irish Republic (402 39901/fax 402 32129 Telex 80461)

ARKLOW RIVER	72	2942	4074	94,7	14,0	5,7	12	cem

(ex Milburn Carrier-89)

Managers for:
Arklow Shipping (Overseas) Ltd

ARKLOW BAY	88	1524	2181	73,9	11,8	4,4	10	gen(31c)
ARKLOW MANOR	87	1524	2181	73,8	11,8	4,4	10	gen(31c)
ARKLOW MARSH	88	1524	2183	73,8	11,8	4,4	10	gen(31c)
ARKLOW MILL	88	1524	2179	73,8	11,8	4,4	10	gen(31c)
ARKLOW MOOR	90	1524	2165	73,9	11,8	4,4	10	gen(31c)

Bay Shipping Ltd

ARKLOW ABBEY	81	1171	1644	70,6	10,8	4,3	10	gen

Coastal Shipping PLC

NISHARK	82	1895	3030	83,8	12,6	5,2	10	gen

(ex Darell-89)

NISHEER	85	1839	2167	78,0	12,7	4,3	11	gen(124c)

(ex Lia Ventura-88, Flagship I-86, Elisa Von Barssel-85)

NISHOWEN	83	1988	3126	77,0	13,2	5,5	10	gen

(ex Raimundo A-88)

Invermore Shipping Ltd

ARKLOW VALE	89	2867	4289	88,2	13,7	5,8	11	gen(173c)
ARKLOW VALLEY	92	2827	4254	88,2	13,7	5,8	11	gen(173c)
ARKLOW VALOUR	90	2827	4258	88,2	13,7	5,8	11	gen(173c)
ARKLOW VENTURE	90	2827	4261	88,2	13,7	5,8	11	gen(173c)
ARKLOW VIEW	90	2827	4261	88,2	13,7	5,8	11	gen(173c)
ARKLOW VIKING	90	2827	4299	88,2	13,7	5,8	11	gen(173c)
ARKLOW VILLA	91	2827	4258	88,3	13,7	5,8	11	gen(173c)

Sailaway Sailor PLC

ARKLOW MEADOW	90	1524	2172	73,8	11,6	4,4	10	gen(31c)

Sheil & Byrne Overseas Ltd

ARKLOW BEACH	76	3663	5662	102,3	15,6	7,0	13	gen

(ex Atlantic Fisher-88, Sandgate-82)

James Tyrrell Ltd

SERENELL	77	999	1632	61,5	10,4	4,8	10	gen
SHEVRELL	81	1891	3033	83,8	12,6	5,2	10	gen
VALZELL	76	999	1608	61,5	10,4	4,8	10	gen

To be bareboat chartered:
Devon Line Ltd

New building	95		7000					bulk
New building	95		7000					bulk

ARKLOW MOOR at Belfast
(Alan Gedde...

BAILEY & BOYNTON MARINE
184A Hessle Road, Hull, HU3 3AD (01964 532409/fax 01964 532409)

SARK TRADER (ex Function-83)	63	196	254	30,4	6,7	2,5	7	gen bg

Note. Laid up

BANKS SEAFARMS LTD.
Coel-na-Mara, St Margaret's Hope, Orkney, KW17 2TL (0856 831226)

LYRAWA BAY (ex Sam-76)	70	101	45	27,1	7,5	3,0	9	r(

BELL LINES LTD.
Bell House, Montague Street, Dublin 2, Irish Rep (1 478 3200/fax 1 478 2121)

Chartered Tonnage:

Partenreederei m.s. "Amazone" Kahler & Sohne KG

AMAZONE	87	2749	3178	94,5	16,1	5,0	14	gen(262c)

KG Schiffahrtsgesellschaft Klaus Jurgens m.s. "Angela Jurgens" mbH & Co

ANGELA JURGENS	88	2749	3146	94,5	16,1	5,0	14	gen(262c)

Reederei Gerd A. Gorke

CORINNA *(a)* (ex Vantage-93, Bell Vantage-78)	74	2130	2450	81,4	13,4	4,9	13	gen(144c)

Partenreederei m.s. "Jan Becker" Bernd Becker KG

JAN BECKER	87	2749	3173	94,5	16,2	5,0	14	gen(262c)

m.s. "Jana" Holgar und Herbert Szidat KG

JANA	90	3125	3000	89,1	16,2	4,8	14	gen(260c)

m.s. "Jan Kahrs" KG

JAN KAHRS	88	2770	3175	94,5	16,1	5,0	14	gen(262c)

Partenreederei m.s. "Otto Becker"

OTTO BECKER	89	2749	3144	94,5	16,1	5,0	14	gen(262c)

K/S Container Ship

ROSITA MARIA *(n)*	77	2316	2600	81,4	13,4	5,0	13	gen(174c)

Unitas Schiffahrts mbH & Co. m.s. "Ady"

ELL ADY	95	2460					14	gen(300c)
ew building	95	2500					14	gen(300c)
ew building	95	2500					14	gen(300c)

ote. Flag - all Germany except (n) - Norway (NIS) (a) - Antigua & Barbuda ; see also EURO
'ONTAINER SHIPPING

BLUE CIRCLE CEMENT LTD.

Iorthfleet Works, The Shore, Northfleet, Kent, DA11 9AN (01474 564 355/fax 01474 535 493)

;LUE CIRCLE NTERPRISE	56	485	850	78,0	8,2	2,4	12	cem bge
;LUE CIRCLE 'ENTURE	55	508	850	78,0	8,2	2,4	12	cem bge

J. BOSTON & SON SHIPPING LTD.

;ayley Road , Oreston, Plymouth, PL9 7NQ (01752 407265)

:ONTRIBUTOR *	60	256	373	42,7	6,6	2,7	7	bk tk bge
(ex Beagle Venturer-73, Kendale H)								

*Vote. * converting for dry cargo*

BP OIL UK LTD.

;hip Management, BP House, Breakspear Way, Hemel Hempstead, Herts, HP2 4UL
01442 232323/fax 01442 225225 Telex 82666 beepeeoil)

3P BATTLER	68	1410	2257	76,0	12,5	4,7	11	tk
(ex Inverness-76)								
3P JOUSTER	72	1568	2734	79,0	12,6	5,2	12	tk
(ex Swansea-76)								
3P SPRINGER	69	1071	1538	65,5	11,3	4,5	11	tk
(ex Dublin-76)								
3P WARRIOR	68	1410	2257	76,0	12,5	4,7	11	tk
(ex Grangemouth-76)								

BP BATTLER at Calshot   *(Colin Drayson)*

BROMLEY SHIPPING PLC

Imperial House, 21-25 North Street, Bromley, Kent, BR1 1SJ (0181 290 0105/fax 0181 464 5609)

BROMLEY PEARL	90	2230	3222	99,7	13,0	4,3	11	gen(114c

See also UNION TRANSPORT

BULLAS TANKCRAFT CO LTD.

Telegraph House, Telegraph Hill, Higham, Rochester, Kent, ME3 7MW (01634 717509/fax 01634 295079)

RAPID II	71	801	1392	69,4	9,0	3,0	11	tk bge
(ex Celtic 4-94, Oiltrans 31-81)								
THAMES RAPID	74	589	670	58,9	10,3	2,6	10	tk bge
(ex Rapid-86, BP Rapid-86, Sheppey-76)								

C.W. SHIPPING LTD.

Fountain Cross, Ennis, Co Clare, Irish Republic (65 29124/fax 65 28316)

MATRISHA	77	999	2250	79,2	12,4	4,8	12	gen (104c
(ex Duisburg-88, Coburg-86, Boberg-84)								

Note. Bahamas flag, laid up damaged

CAMPBELL MARITIME LTD.

Maritime House, 6, Coronation Street, South Shields, Tyne & Wear, NE33 1LA
(0191 427 0303/fax 0191 455 0790 Telex 537406cammia)

Managers for:

Baltship IoM Ltd

CT SUN (o)	80	3829	4641	96,8	15,5	6,6	13	ch tk
(ex Coppelia-92)								

CASU Investments Ltd

CAROLE T	80	499	1120	50,0	9,5	3,9	9	gen
(ex Emily PG-93)								

Celtic Tankers PLC

CELTIC TERRIER	79	7676	12905	142,4	17,8	8,6	14	ch tk
(ex United Terrier-93, Ilse-91)								
PAMELA C	78	499	1056	50,0	10,0	3,9	9	gen
(ex Alice PG-91)								

CT Shipmanagement IoM Ltd

CT STAR (o)	81	6060	870	129,6	19,4	7,0	14	tk
(ex Sulphur-87, Stena Sulphur-87, OT Sulphur-83)								

Forth Tankers PLC

FORTH BRIDGE	92	3338	5800	96,2	16,1	6,6	12	tk

Franco British Chartering Agency Ltd

ARDENT	83	498	1180	50,0	9,5	3,6	9	gen
CORNET (b)	76	796	1255	64,0	10,5	3,8	11	gen(52c
(ex Daunt Rock-88)								
MILLAC STAR II (b)	74	500	1535	75,7	11,8	3,9	12	gen
(ex Emanaich-86, Caravelle-83)								
ROUSTEL (b)	78	797	1240	64,0	10,5	3,7	11	gen(52c
(ex Skellig Rock-88)								
TORRENT	91	999	1733	53,8	11,0	4,1	9	gen

Note. Flag - (o) - IoM (b) - Bahamas

CARISBROOKE SHIPPING PLC.

10 Mill Hill Road, Cowes, Isle of Wight, PO31 7EA (01983 299244 /fax 01983 290111 Telex 86771 caship)

CHERYL C	83	1597	2467	70,1	13,1	5,0	10	gen(70c)
(ex Catarina Caldas-91, Catarina-89, Norbrit Rijn-87, Norbrit Hope-85)								
GRETA C	74	1599	2628	77,8	13,2	5,0	12	gen
(ex Mairi Everard-90)								
HELEEN C	74	1463	2159	71,3	11,6	5,0	12	gen
(ex Luther-89, Irina-81)								
KLAZINA C	83	1633	2554	81,3	12,0	4,3	10	gen
(ex Lasina-88, Klazina H-88, Klazina-85)								
MARK C	71	1596	2823	85,0	12,8	5,1	13	gen
(ex Mark-86, Security-86)								

MARK C at Belfast　　　　　　　　　　　　　　　　　　*(Alan Geddes)*

MARY C	77	1432	2440	66,1	13,1	5,1	12	gen
(ex Fiducia-89, Ligato-88)								
NATACHA C	82	1597	2467	70,0	13,1	3,4	10	gen(70c)
(ex Natacha Caldas-91, Natacha-89, Norbrit Maas-87, Norbrit Faith-85)								
VANESSA C	74	1853	3165	80,1	13,6	5,5	12	gen
(ex Vanessa-93)								

Bareboat charter :
Scheepswerf Damen B.V.

NORDSTRAND *(a)*	91	1960	2800	88,3	12,5	4,6	11	gen(158c)
(ex Nicole-93)								

Managers for:
MARTESE (Marine Technical Services) Ltd

ANJA C *(j)*	91	2230	3222	99,7	13,0	4,3	11	gen(114c)
(ex Tima Saturn 92, Launched as Union Saturn)								

Vectis Shipping Ltd. (Carisbrooke Shipping/James Fisher & Son)

VECTIS FALCON	78	2351	3564	87,0	13,8	5,7	12	gen
(ex Fribourg-93, Clarknes-83)								
VECTIS ISLE	90	2230	3222	99,7	13,0	4,3	11	gen(114c)
(ex Lesley-Jane C-93, completed as Union Mercury)								

Note.   All Barbados flag except (a) - Antigua & Barbuda (j) - St Vincent & the Grenadines

CIVIL & MARINE LTD.

Johnson's Wharf, King Edward Road, Greenhithe, Kent, DA9 9AD
(01322 384646/fax 01322 387211 Telex 896020civmar)

CAMBROOK	82	2318	3020	99,8	11,4	4,3	10	gen(100c
(ex Lena Wessels-87)								

Note. Bahamas flag

CLIFFGOLD LTD.

trading as N. E. MURRAY MARINE CONTRACTORS,
8 Rushenden Road, Queenborough , Kent, ME11 5BH (01795 580998/fax 01795 665534)

CAPTION	63	189	269	32,1	7,2	2,3	8	sanc
ISLAND SWALLOW *	75	499	800	42,5	10,0	3,6	9	ger
(ex Sealand Trader-87)								
LIBATION +	69	198	300	30,6	6,9	2,6	8	sanc
MARGARET G	15	162	265	33,5	6,4	2,2	9	sand
(ex Sidney P-87, Sway-64, X-Lighter)								
NICHOLA G	15	172	254	33,5	6,4	2,6	8	sand
(ex Colin P-87, Leah P-73, Betty Hudson-64, X-Lighter)								
SEACOMBE TRADER	74	480	711	42,5	10,0	4,2	9	gen bge

*Note. * Laid up repairing + to be renamed KAREN G*

COASTAL CONTAINER LINE LTD.

S.6 Berth, Royal Seaforth Container Terminal, Seaforth, Liverpool, L21 1JD
(0151 949-1000/fax 0151 949-10079)

Chartered tonnage:

Partenreederei m.s. "Johanna"								
JOHANNA (s)	91	3125	2973	89,1	16,2	4,9	14	gen(258c)
Reederei Klaus Schneider KG								
KIRSTEN (a)	83	2046	1876	78,0	13,9	5,0	13	gen(124c)
(ex Christopher Caribe-93, Saturnus-92, Craigavad-88)								
Partenreederei m.s. "Neptunus"								
NEPTUNUS (s)	83	2046	1880	78,0	13,9	5,0	13	gen(124c)
(ex Craigantlet-88)								
m.s. "Sybille" Reederei Ludtke KG								
SYBILLE (s)	91	3125	2973	89,1	16,2	4,8	14	gen(260c)
(ex Baltic Bridge-93, Sybille-93)								

Note. Flag - (a) - Antigua & Barbuda (s) - Germany

COE METCALF SHIPPING LTD.

6th Floor, Martins Building, Water Street, Liverpool, L2 3UJ
(0151 227-5531/fax 0151 236-2269 Telex 629427ships)

BRIARTHORN	80	1483	2435	74,6	12,9	4,9	12	gen
(ex Craigallian-89)								
DAVID M	80	2077	3120	82,0	15,0	5,8	14	oil/ch tk
(ex BP Harrier-91)								
FRANK M	65	1307	1819	70,7	11,4	4,8	11	tk
FREDERICK M	80	1594	2924	75,2	13,3	5,8	12	tk
GORDON THOMAS	64	915	1299	70,1	10,4	4,3	11	oil/bit tk
(ex Salineke-90, Salaria-80)								
JOHN M	63	1308	1839	70,1	11,4	4,8	11	tk
MICHAEL M	80	2077	3120	82,0	15,0	5,8	14	oil/ch tk
(ex BP Hunter-91)								
NICHOLAS M	65	1308	1819	70,7	11,4	4,8	11	tk

REDTHORN	78	2025	3070	85,3	13,8	5,0	12	gen
(ex Pinewood-90)								
ROBERT M	70	1675	2449	85,0	12,8	4,4	11	oil/bit tk
(ex Cree-77)								
ROSETHORN	82	995	1694	69.3	11,1	4,3	11	gen(60c)
(ex Shamrock Endeavour-90)								
SILVERTHORN	82	995	1694	69,3	11,1	4,3	11	gen(60c)
(ex Shamrock Enterprise-90)								

Note. The company is a wholly owned subsidiary of JAMES FISHER & SONS PLC *qv*

SILVERTHORN at Belfast   (Alan Geddes)

COMMODORE FERRIES LTD.

Commodore House, PO Box 10, Bulwer Avenue, St Sampson, Guernsey, C.I. , GY1 3AF
(01481 46841/fax 01481 49543 Telex 4191401)

ISLAND COMMODORE	May 95	7300	5215	126,4	21,0	6,0	18	ro
New building	Mar 96	7300		126,4	21,0	6,0	18	ro

Time chartered:
  Clare Business Ltd

NORMAN COMMODORE *(b)*	72	6040	2677	109,5	20,4	4,9	18	ro(200c)

  (ex Pride of Portsmouth-91, Mads Mols-89, Mols Trader-87, Merchant Trader-87, Sir Lamorak-86,
  Lakespan Ontario-83, Lady Catherine-81, Lune Bridge-80, Anu-80, Norcliff-74, Anu-73)
  Christiania Eiendomsselskap A/S

COMMODORE CLIPPER *(n)*	71	6136	4171	118,4	16,1	6,0	14	ro(218c)

  (ex Euro Nor-91, Misidi-90, Normandia-86, Juno-79)
  Channel Island Ship Management Ltd

PURBECK *(b)*	78	6507	1550	125,5	17,5	4,5	18	ro

Note. Flag - (b) - Bahamas   (n) - Norway (NIS)

C. CRAWLEY LTD.

Town Pier, West Street, Gravesend, Kent, DA11 0BN

(01474 365244 /fax 01474 320673 Telex 965672crawly)

AQUADUCT	64	594	908	62,3	10,2	3,0	10	tk bge
(ex Charcrest-91)								
AQUATIC	63	199	315	35,1	7,5	2,3	7	wt tk bge
(ex Busby-85)								
ARTEMISIUM	64	299	520	55,0	6,6	2,5	10	tk bge
BRUCE STONE	64	357	375	43,7	9,2	2,3	8	tk bge
(ex Viaduct-78, Bruce Stone-76)								
DOVERIAN	70	913	1435	69,8	10,0	4,2	11	tk
(ex Whitdale-94,Danae-88, Pass of Chisholm-84, Cordene-75)								
FULFORD	60	477	522	50,3	10,2	2,6	10	tk
(ex Charmo-91)								
MARPOL	57	200	360	36,6	6,5	2,6	8	tk
PERFECTO	67	652	1008	59,2	10,7	3,2	9	tk bge
(ex Shell Driver-89, Perfecto-79)								
TOMMY	63	217	315	35,1	7,5	2,3	8	tk bge
(ex Batsman-87)								
TORDUCT	59	65	100	28,1	5,3	2,1	8	tk
(ex Wakefield-70)								
Managers for:								
Crawley Shipping Ltd								
K/TOULSON (h)	66	614	833	52,9	10,3	3,8	9	tk
(ex Beechcroft-90)								

Note.   (h) - Honduras flag

CRESCENT SHIPPING LTD.

Hays House, Otterham Quay Lane, Rainham, Gillingham, Kent, ME8 7UN
(01634 360077/fax 01634 387500 Telex 96276)

AMBIENCE (b)	83	644	1000	59,6	9,3	3,4	10	gen
BANWELL	80	999	1710	71,9	11,1	3,7	10	tk
BECKENHAM	80	825	1165	64,2	11,5	3,3	11	tk
BLACKHEATH	80	751	1230	60,0	11,3	3,4	11	tk
BOISTERENCE (b)	83	644	1000	59,6	9,3	3,4	10	gen
BRENTWOOD	80	994	1640	69,8	11,3	3,8	11	tk
CRESCENCE (b)	82	644	1000	59,6	9,3	3,3	10	gen
KINDRENCE (b)	76	1596	3210	91,2	13,5	5,1	10	gen
LUMINENCE (b)	77	1928	3210	91,3	13,5	5,1	10	gen
PIQUENCE (b)	79	945	1452	72,5	11,3	3,3	10	gen
QUIESCENCE (b)	79	945	1452	72,3	11,3	3,3	10	gen
STRIDENCE (b)	83	698	1821	84,7	11,5	3,5	10	gen
TARQUENCE (b)	80	644	1000	59,6	9,3	3,4	10	gen
TURBULENCE (b)	83	699	1821	84,8	11,5	3,5	10	gen
URGENCE (b)	81	699	1842	84,8	11,5	3,4	10	gen
VIBRENCE (b)	81	699	1842	84,8	11,5	3,4	10	gen
Managers for:								
Lloyds Equipment Leasing Ltd								
BLACKFRIARS	85	992	1570	69,9	11,1	3,8	10	tk
Lloyds Industrial Leasing Ltd								
BREAKSEA	85	992	1570	69,9	11,3	3,8	10	tk
Lloyds International Leasing Ltd								
BLACKROCK	89	1646	2675	78,5	12,7	4,9	10	tk

TARQUENCE inward bound in the River Ouse   *(David H. Smith)*

Lloyds Leasing (North Sea Transport) Ltd

BARDSEY *(b)*	81	1144	1767	69,5	11,8	4,3	10	tk
(ex Sten-86)								
BARMOUTH	80	1144	1774	69,5	11,8	4,3	10	tk
(ex Per-86)								

Lloyds Plant Leasing Ltd

BRABOURNE	89	1646	2675	78,5	12,7	4,9	10	tk

Note.   (b) - Bahamas flag

CRESCENT SHIP MANAGEMENT LTD

Hays House, Otterham Quay Lane, Rainham, Gillingham, Kent, ME8 7UN
(01634 360077/fax 01634 387500 Telex 96276)

Managers for:
City Leasing (Teeside) Ltd

THAMES	77	2663	2936	93,3	15,1	4,6	12	sludge

Thames Water Utilities Ltd

BEXLEY	66	2175	2471	89,9	15,1	4,1	12	sludge
HOUNSLOW	68	2132	2471	89,9	15,2	4,1	12	sludge

JOHN DEAN

10 Wentworth Way, Hull, North Humberside, HU9 2AX (01482 219277)

GEORGE ODEY	71	210	300	37,7	6,7	2,4	7	gen bge

DEAN & DYBALL SHIPPING LTD.

Ocean House, New Quay Road, Poole, Dorset, BH15 4AB
(01202 665665/fax 01202 678074 Telex 418287ddship)

DOUGLAS McWILLIAM	83	172	200	30,3	8,1	2,1	7	eff tk
REEDNESS	68	500	1221	60,6	10,3	4,2	11	eff tk
(ex Kyndill II-86, Kyndill-85, Gerda Brodsgaard-73)								
TRENTAIRE	56	285	450	54,9	5,1	3,1	8	eff tk
(ex Languedoc-87)								
TRENTCAL	56	285	450	54,9	5,1	3,1	8	eff tk
(ex Auvergne-87)								

DENVAL MARINE CONSULTANTS LTD.

156 High Street, Sevenoaks, Kent, TN13 1XE (01732 458288/fax 01732 458277 Telex 888066denval)

Managers for:
Larkspur Maritime Co Ltd

FLEUR DE LYS	82	2763	5273	122,8	18,3	6,4	17	ro(284c)
(ex Lux Expressway-88, Roll Galicia-88)								

Chartwell Navigation Co Ltd

ROSEANNE	82	7744	4106	112,8	18,7	6,4	14	ro(100c)
(ex Faroy-89, Reina del Cantabrico-87, Salah Labiad-85, Reina del Cantabrico-83)								

Poseidon Schiffahrt OHG

ROSEBAY	76	13700	5233	135,5	21,8	6,1	17	ro(248c)
(ex Transgermania-93)								

Note. All Cyprus flag

DOOLIN FERRY CO LTD.

Doolin Pier, Doolin, Co Clare, Irish Republic (65 74455)

PALBRO PRIDE	64	200	367	41,6	7,7	2,3	8	gen
(ex Milligan-81, Lady Serena-87)								

ONESIMUS DOREY (SHIPOWNERS) LTD.

La Salerie House, St Peter Port, PO Box 33, Guernsey, C.I. (01481 56605/fax 01481 53450)
Note. The company is a wholly owned subsidiary of JAMES FISHER & SONS PLC . *See also*
AGRITRANS, DUNDALK SHIPOWNERS, F. T. EVERARD, SWINSHIP MANAGEMENT, TORBULK

DRAGON SHIPPING LINE

F Berth, King's Dock, Swansea, West Glamorgan,SA1 (01792 458854/fax 01792 456605)

Agents only for:
Bahamian Steamship Corp

KENMARE	*(a)*	68	2435	2290	86,8	14,6	4,6	14	gen(88c)
(ex Kantone-87, Hermia-87, Marietta Bolten-74)									

H. Boeree

MERCATOR	*(d)*	71	499	1370	76,3	11,9	3,9	13	gen(136 c)
(ex Lautonia-89, Heinrich Knuppel-85)									

Note. Flag - (a) - Antigua & Barbuda (d) - Netherlands

KENMARE at Belfast   (Alan Geddes)

DUBLIN MARITIME LTD.

Maritime House, North Wall, Dublin 1, Irish Republic (1 874 1231/ fax 1 872 5714)

Chartered tonnage:
    D-Line Shipping Co Ltd m.v. "Mathilde"

MATHILDE *(a)*	94	3958	5400	108,0	16,0	6,0	16	gen(448c)

    (Launched as Dorte)
    m.s. "Merkur" Reederei G. Bartels K.G.

MERKUR *(s)*	91	3815	4155	103,5	16,3	6,1	14	gen(372c)

Note. Flag - (a) - Antigua & Barbuda (s) - Germany

DUBLIN SHIPPING LTD.

6 Beechill, Clonskeagh, Dublin 4, Irish Republic (1 2696477/fax1 2839361 Telex 93793celd)

RATHROWAN	91	2920	4059	96,0	14,4	5,9	12	oil/bit tk
Managers for:								
Kyle Shipping Ltd								
RATHKYLE	81	8185	14037	135,0	19,4	9,2	13	oil/ch tk
(ex Rich Star-87)								
Lynn Shipping Ltd								
RATHLYNN	78	3978	6902	105,6	16,3	7,1	13	oil/ch tk
(ex Rich Crane-81)								
Moy Shipping Ltd								
RATHMOY	82	4157	6994	95,9	17,4	7,4	12	oil/veg tk
(ex Tomoe 63-83)								
Rathnew Shipping Ltd								
RATHNEW	78	1591	3165	93,2	13,8	5,3	13	oil/bit tk

RATHKYLE in the estuary of the River Elbe *(Barry Standerline)*

DUNDALK SHIPOWNERS LTD.

4 Jocelyn Court, Dundalk, Co Louth, Irish Republic (42 39320/fax 42 26623)

Managers for;
Onesimus Dorey (Shipowners) Ltd, demise chartered to Dundalk Shipowners Ltd

ROCKFLEET	79	999	1622	66,2	11,5	4,5	11	gen
(ex Globe-93)								
ROCKISLAND	78	492	1467	80,4	10,1	3,3	11	gen(47c)
(ex Verena-92)								
ROCKPOINT	77	1597	2703	73,3	13,2	5,1	11	gen
(ex Arklow Valley-91, Procyon-84)								

ROCKABILL leaving Dublin *(Courtesy of Dundalk Shipowners Ltd.)*

SEA AVON *	77	1102	2273	69,0	13,5	4,5	9	gen

Irish Continental Group PLC (IRISH FERRIES)

ROCKABILL	84	3329	4115	98,7	15,5	5,4	14	gen(332c)

(ex Hasselwerder-94, Gracechurch Crown-90, Hasselwerder-89, City of Manchester-85, Hasselwerder-84)

Tiree Chartering (Dundalk Shipowners/McCorkell Shipping) managers for:

McCorkell Shipping Ltd

ROCKFORD	76	956	1588	65,8	10,9	4,3	12	gen

(ex Canford-94, Viscount-88)

Dundalk Shipowners Ltd

ROCQUAINE (b)	77	985	1559	66,9	10,8	4,1	11	gen(58c)

Note.   (b) - Bahamas flag   *   Time chartered to SEACON LTD qv
See also AGRI-TRANS

EASDALE ISLAND SHIPPING LINE

Norton Curlew Manor, Hatton, Warwick, CV35 8XQ (01926 842227/fax 01926 843314)

EILEAN EISDEAL	44	96	138	20,3	5,6	2,0	7	gen

(ex Eldesa-84, VIC 72)

Managers for:

Elcon Finans A/S

EILEAN DUBH E	92	368	137	40,3	10,6	2,7	9	gen(17c)

(ex Sun Truck-94)

EFFLUENTS SERVICES LTD.

140 Moss Lane, Macclesfield, Cheshire, SK11, 7YT (01625 429666/fax 01625 511305 Telex 667737effie)

ALSTON	68	836	1493	61,6	10,0	4,2	11	eff tk
(ex Leadsman-85)								
GREENDALE H	62	311	536	43,1	6,7	3,1	7	eff tk
HAWESWATER	68	1469	1575	78,5	12,6	4,0	12	eff tk

(ex Percy Dawson-88)

ALSTON in the River Ouse off Goole   (Richard Potter)

EURO CONTAINER SHIPPING PLC (ECS)

Dolphin House, 1 Georges Street, Waterford, Irish Republic(51 78922/fax 51 73032 Telex 80554bshp)

BELL PIONEER	90	6111	4833	114,5	18,9	5,9	14	cc(303c)▸
BELL RACER	77	1936	3342	92,0	13,5	5,2	13	gen(168c)▸
BELL RULER	77	1936	3342	92,0	13,5	5,2	13	gen(168c)▸
EURO POWER	92	6455	5334	118,0	17,2	7,5	14	cc(378c)▸

(ex OOCL Shanghai-94, Euro Power-93)

Managers for:

Swift Navigation Co Ltd

BELL RANGER	76	1949	3340	92,8	13,5	5,3	13	gen(168c)

Reederei Gerd A. Gorke

BELL SWIFT (a)	76	1599	3850	93,5	14,5	6,1	14	gen(205c)

(ex Jan-91, Arfell-90, Jan-87)

Note. (a) - Antigua & Barbuda flag ; see also BELL LINES

F. T. EVERARD & SONS LTD.

The Wharf, Greenhithe, Kent, DA9 9NW (01322 382345/fax 01322 383422 Telex 21519evrard)

ABILITY	79	1409	2550	79,3	13,2	5,0	13	oil/veg tk
AUTHENTICITY	79	1409	2550	79,3	13,2	4,9	12	oil/veg tk
SAGACITY (b)	73	1926	3238	91,3	13,3	5,1	12	gen
SPECIALITY (b)	77	2822	4245	89,7	14,3	6,0	12	gen(122c)
STABILITY (b)	78	2822	4245	91,1	14,3	6,4	12	gen(122c)

Managers for:

F. T. Everard Shipping Ltd

AGILITY	90	1930	3144	80,0	14,6	5,6	11	tk
ALACRITY	90	1930	3000	80,0	14,6	5,6	12	tk
AMITY (b)	80	1098	1767	69,5	11,8	4,3	11	tk

(ex Christian-88)

AVERITY (b)	81	1144	1770	69,5	11,8	4,3	11	tk

(ex Natalie-88)

SPECIALITY in the Bristol Channel

(Iain McCall)

SANGUITY	84	1892	2415	79,0	12,7	4,6	10	gen(94c)
(ex Willonia-88)								
SOCIALITY	86	1892	2415	79,0	12,8	4,6	10	gen(94c)
(ex Stevonia-87)								
Hadley Shipping Co Ltd								
COTINGA (b)	76	1921	3089	83,5	14,1	5,2	11	gen
Scottish Navigation Co Ltd								
SENIORITY	91	3493	5163	99,5	16,6	5,4	11	gen
SUPERIORITY	91	2230	3212	100,0	12,4	4,3	11	gen(114c)
Short Sea Europe PLC								
NORTH SEA TRADER	91	2230	3222	99,7	12,4	4,3	11	gen(114c)
RIVER TRADER	82	1859	2607	88,5	12,2	4,1	11	gen(108c)
(launched as Sea Trader)								
SHORT SEA TRADER	91	2230	3263	99,7	12,4	4,3	10	gen(114c)
3i PLC								
AMENITY	80	1453	2528	79,2	13,2	5,0	13	tk
PAMELA EVERARD	84	1892	2415	79,0	12,7	4,6	10	gen(94c)
SELECTIVITY	84	1892	2415	79,0	12,7	4,6	10	gen(94c)

Note.   (b) - Bahamas flag

PAMELA EVERARD arriving at Belfast

(Alan Geddes)

F. T. EVERARD & SONS MANAGEMENT LTD.

4 Elder Street, London, E1 6DD (0171 247-8181/fax 0171 377-5562 Telex 887230everad)

Agents for:

Apollo Ships Ltd

CELEBRITY	76	663	946	57,6	10,0	3,3	10	gen

Onesimus Dorey (Shipowners) Ltd, demise chartered to Mount Bridge Shipping Ltd,Boston

CITY	76	559	880	56,1	9,9	3,2	10	gen

Onesimus Dorey (Shipowners) Ltd, demise chartered to Torbulk Ltd, Grimsby

PENTLAND	80	909	1315	60,0	11,3	3,9	12	gen
(ex Capacity-94, Lizzonia-89)								
PORTLAND	80	909	1315	60,0	11,3	3,9	11	gen
(ex Comity-94, Angelonia-88)								

Faversham Ships Ltd

CONFORMITY	75	559	880	56,1	9,9	3,2	11	gen

D. J. Goubert Shipping Ltd

CANDOURITY	75	559	880	56,1	9,9	3,2	10	gen
LANCRESSE	78	664	953	57,5	10.1	3,4	11	gen
(ex Bressay Sound-94, Edgar Dorman-89)								

LANCRESSE leaving Birkenhead, with a familiar Mersey backdrop   *(Ambuscade Marine Photography)*

FALMOUTH OIL SERVICES (1994) LTD.

The Docks, Falmouth, Cornwall, TR11 4NJ (01326 211333/fax 01326 312989)

FALMOUTH ENDEAVOUR	72	607	1276	62,7	9,8	4,2	11	bk tk
(ex Marwah II-87)								
FALMOUTH ENTERPRISE	72	1287	2189	76,0	11,2	5,1	11	bk tk
(ex Brady Maria-87, Hama Maru No 5-84)								

Chartered tonnage:
  John H. Whitaker (Tankers) Ltd

FALMOUTH ENDURANCE	64	171	420	45,2	6,0	2,1	9	tk bge
(ex Humber Navigator-89)								
FALMOUTH ENERGY	63	165	275	42,1	5,3	2,1	7	tk bge
(ex Rufus Stone-89)								
FALMOUTH INDUSTRY	61	257	500	44,0	6,3	2,4	8	tk bge
(ex Ulster Industry-89)								

FERRYLINK FREIGHT SERVICE

Ferry Terminal, Sheerness, Kent, ME12 1RX (01795 581600/fax 01795 581700)

Chartered tonnage:
  The Egyptian Navigation Co (ENC)

AL HUSSEIN	85	2039	3133	112,7	17,9	5,3	17	ro(257c)
(ex Nuweiba-85)								
NUWAYBA	89	2039	3094	101,1	17,5	5,2	17	ro(236c)
(ex Nuweiba-93)								

Note. Both Egypt flag - operate as FERRYLINK MEDWAY *&* FERRYLINK SCHELDT *resp*

W. FIELDGATE & SON LTD.

Haven Quay, Colchester, Essex, CO2 8JE (01206 865432/fax 01206 866104 Telex 98126fldgte)

Agents only for:
  Seatrade Ltd

RAIDER	66	200	378	41,6	7,7	2,3	8	gen
(ex Anglian Trader-90, Lee James-82, Target Venture-78, Sheena K-78, Lady Sheena-76)								

Note. St Vincent & the Grenadines flag

FINN VALLEY OIL

Castlefinn, Co Donegal, Irish Republic (74 46274)

FINN VALLEY OIL	47	198	203	30,5	7,0	2,4	8	bk tk bge
(ex Sure Hand-89, Rinso-75)								

JAMES FISHER & SONS PLC.

Fisher House, PO Box 4, Barrow-in-Furness, Cumbria, LA14 1HR
(01229 822323/fax 01229 836761 Telex 65163fisher)

ABERTHAW FISHER	66	2330	2233	86,6	16,5	4,6	11	ro h/l
(ex National Generation-92, Aberthaw Fisher-90)								
FURNESS FISHER	55	1721	2464	97,5	11,9	2,6	9	bk tk bge
(ex Nordicus One-89)								
NEW GENERATION	66	2330	2233	86,7	16,5	4,6	11	ro h/l
(ex Kingsnorth Fisher-90)								

Managers for:
British Nuclear Fuels Ltd
EUROPEAN

SHEARWATER	81	2486	1583	80,0	12,6	5,1	11	nuc
(ex Mediterranean Shearwater-94)								

Note. ONESIMUS DOREY (SHIPOWNERS) LTD *and* COE METCALF SHIPPING LTD *are wholly owned subsidiary companies. See also* STEPHENSON CLARKE *and* CARISBROOKE SHIPPING

NEW GENERATION heading west in the Bristol Channel

(Bernard McCall)

K. G. FISSER & v. DOORNUM GmbH & CO.

Feldbrunnenstrasse 43-45, 20148 Hamburg, Germany (040 44186241/fax 040 445686 Telex 212671fido)

Managers for:
Alsace Shipping Co Ltd

KELLS *(c)*	77	1986	2657	79,2	12,4	4,7	10,5	gen(104c)
(ex Gotaland-88)								
Athlacca Ltd								
KILLARNEY *(i)*	77	1289	2908	96,3	12,4	4,8	12	gen(207c)
(ex Anholt-86, Neuwerk-81)								

Kinsale Shipping Co Ltd

KENMARE *(c)*	75	5306	8110	117,6	18,1	7,2	14	bulk
(ex Raute-86, Singapura-83, Raute-78)								
KINSALE *(c)*	76	5306	8150	117,6	18,1	7,3	15	bulk(170c)
(ex Rhombus-86, Wachau-84, Bayu-83, Rhombus-78)								

Note.   Flag - (c) - Cyprus (i) - Irish Rep

FRODSHAM LIGHTERAGE CO.

9 Poulton Green Close, Spital, Bebington, Wirral, L63 9FC (0151 334 6715/fax 0151 334 6715)

PANARY	37	167	260	29,5	6,5	2,6	8	gen bge

J. & A. GARDNER & CO LTD.

36 Washington Street, Glasgow, G3 8AZ (0141 221-7845/fax 0141 204-2388 Telex 77205gardnr)

SAINT BRANDAN	76	931	1394	63,8	10,8	4,1	10	ro/gen
SAINT KEARAN	78	441	775	50,4	9,1	3,3	9	ch tk
SAINT ORAN	81	573	719	53,3	9,2	3,4	10	ro/ch tk

J. & A. GARDNER & CO (MANAGEMENT) LTD.

Details as above

Managers for:
Golden Sea Produce Ltd

SOLEA	89	235	326	33,5	7,6	3,4	8	fish

SOLEA at Oban

(Iain McCall)

GARDSCREEN SHIPPING LTD.

2 Norreys Road, Rainham, Gillingham, Kent, ME8 9NJ (01634 377177/fax 01634 377177 Telex 96379gardsc)

CLEO	70	199	429	41,8	7,7	2,7	9	gen
(ex Kali-94, Sealight-93, Wis-77)								
GINO *(h)*	69	391	580	44,4	7,9	3,1	9	gen
(ex Ambience-82)								
HOLM SOUND	69	392	609	44,4	7,9	3,2	9	gen
(ex Gore-87, Eloquence-85)								
JOHNO	61	249	414	42,0	7,6	2,4	8	gen
(ex Ahmed Issa-92, Bandick-90, Christine-74)								

Note. (h) - Honduras flag

GRACECHURCH LINE LTD.

2nd Floor, Port of Liverpool Buildings, Pier Head, Liverpool, L21 1BZ (0151 231-1144/fax 0151 231 1375)

Chartered tonnage:

Unitas Schiffahrtsges mbH & Co m.s. "German" KG

GERMAN	92	3585	4150	99,9	16,3	5,4	15	gen(325c)
(ex Jork-93)								

Reedereiges m.s. "Komet" Henry Gerdau KG GmbH & Co

GRACECHURCH

COMET	90	4169	4752	11,1	16,1	6,0	15	gen(378c)
(ex Komet III-91)								

m.s. "Zenit" Bernd Bartels KG

GRACECHURCH

CROWN	91	3815	4665	103,6	16,2	6,1	14	gen(372c)
(ex Zenit-91)								

m.s. "Sven Dede" Friedhelm Dede KG

GRACECHURCH HARP	91	3815	4659	103,5	16,0	6,1	14	gen(372c)
(completed as Sven Dede)								

Herman Buss KG m.s. "Western Trader"

GRACECHURCH

METEOR *(a)*	91	4164	4744	111,1	16,1	6,0	14	gen(381c)
(completed as Western Trader)								

Claus Markus Speck KG

GRACECHURCH

PLANET	91	3815	4660	103,5	16,2	6,7	14	gen(372c)
(ex Nordic Bridge-94, ECL Commander-91, Schleswig Holstein-91)								

Note. Flag - all Germany except (a) - Antigua & Barbuda

GENCHEM MARINE LTD.

Maritime House, 19A St Helens Street, Ipswich, Suffolk, IP4 1HE
(01473 231121/fax 01473 232265 Telex 987379genmar)

Managers for:

Breydon Marine Ltd

BREYDON

ENTERPRISE	79	498	1046	45,7	9,5	3,9	9	gen
(ex Wib-87)								

BREYDON

VENTURE	77	491	1036	45,9	10,0	3,9	9	gen
(ex Wis-86)								

Cleverpitch Ltd

BURE *(p)*	69	365	610	44,4	7,9	3,2	9	gen
(ex Cadence-85)								

BREYDON VENTURE heading up the River Ouse   *(David H. Smith)*

Ortac Naviera S.A.

TIA *(p)*	64	465	765	50,3	8,8	3,5	9	gen

(ex Elmham-92, Pekari-89, Trostan-81, Northgate-79)

Parkside Warehousing & Transport

BORELLY *	71	507	905	55,7	9,9	3,3	10	gen

(ex Jana Weston-84)

Tora Sea Services Ltd

TORA *(j)*	69	400	713	53,1	8,8	3,3	10	gen

(ex Domba-88, Hoomoss-87, Kosmos-79, Apollo II-70)

James Wiseman

NAUTIC W *(j)*	71	476	646	49,4	8,8	3,1	9	gen

(ex Roy Clemo-86, Commodore Trader-81)

Worthtake Ltd

FORDONNA	72	499	905	55,8	9,9	3,3	10	gen

*Note. Flag - (p) - Panama   (j) - St Vincent & the Grenadines   * Laid up repairing*

GENERAL PORT SERVICES

58-61 Cannons Workshop, Cannons Drive, West India Dock, London, E14 9SU
(0171 5379331/2/fax 0171 5379333)

CONOCOAST	68	209	330	35,4	7,6	3,0	8	bk tk bge
(ex Surehand-92, Bouncer-89)								
CONOSTREAM	61	135	240	39,6	5,1	2,3	8	wt tk bge
DELSTOR	57	155	260	42,0	5,3	2,1	7	tk bge
GOODHAND	64	215	305	35,7	8,1	2,1	8	tk bge
(ex BP Sprite-84, Torksey-76)								

GEORGE GIBSON & CO LTD.

11 John's Place, Leith, Edinburgh, EH6 7EL
(0131 554-4466/fax 0131 555-0310 & 554-0785 Telex 727492anchor)

Managers for:
Gas Shipping & Transport (Jersey) Ltd

TEVIOT	(l)	89	7260	9422	132,2	18,0	8,6	17	lpg
Gibson Gas Tankers Ltd									
QUENTIN	(f)	77	1596	2088	76,1	12,4	5,4	12	lpg
(ex Pentland Moor-79)									
TRAQUAIR	(l)	82	5992	7230	113,8	18,4	8,1	16	lpg
Lloyds Machinery Leasing Ltd									
ETTRICK	(l)	91	3023	3621	88,0	14,9	6,0	13	lpg
LANRICK	(l)	92	3023	3620	88,0	14,9	6,0	14	lpg

Note. Flag - (l) - Liberia (f) - Hong Kong

G. T. GILLIE & BLAIR LTD.

178 New Bridge Street, Newcastle upon Tyne, NE1 2TE
(0191 232-3431/fax 0191 232-8255 Telex 53344gillie)

Managers for:
Ensign Express Shipping Ltd

RIVER DART	81	536	825	50,0	9,3	3,4	10	gen

Note. Gillie & Blair are commercial managers for other dry cargo vessels

GLENLIGHT MANX LTD.

Cumbrae House, Market Street, Douglas, IoM (01624 663395/fax 01624 662033)

GLENFYNE	82	403	460	48,4	8,5	3,0	10	gen
(ex Lille-Birgit-89)								

Managers for:
Clyde Shipping Co Ltd

GLENROSA	80	1082	1452	64,7	11,2	4,0	10	ro/gen
(ex Saint Angus-94)								

Note. Both IoM flag

GROVEFIELD FINANCE LTD.

London

CARMEL	71	199	411	41,8	7,7	2,7	9	gen
(ex Valour-93, Subro Valour-91, Ferryhill II-78)								

Note. Honduras flag Laid up repairing

HAGGERSTONE MARINE LTD.

2A Fanshawe Crescent, Hornchurch, Essex, RM11 2DD
(01708 458695/fax 01708 477349Telex 918001hagger)

Managers for:
Kalafrana Marina Ltd

VEGLIO *(m)*	70	1250	1863	77,3	12,3	4,8	10	ed oil tk

(ex Sandsnipe-94, Litrix-91, Nitrico-79)
Kalkara Shipping Ltd

SYNDIC *(m)*	64	732	1135	61,9	10,0	3,7	11	ed oil tk

(ex Maya-85, Yorksand-77, Pollux-76, Dominentia-76, Mobil Wedel-76, Yorksand-72)
Balena Marine Ltd

DORIS I *(p)*	64	737	877	64,8	9,9	3,5	10	ed oil tk

(ex Doris-81)
Note. Flag - (m) - Malta (p) - Panama
Europa House, 40 South Street, Gt Yarmouth, Norfolk, NR30 2RL

HALCYON SHIPPING LTD.

(01493 856831/fax 01493 857533 Telex 97477halcha) (also at 19 London Road North, Lowestoft, Suffolk)

Agents only for:
Herbert Trading Ltd

REMA *(h)*	56	649	985	56,0	9,0	3,8	10	gen

(ex Don-92, Alpha-89, Ralph-89, Alpha-88, Star-68)
Tara Shipping Ltd

ELLEN W *(j)*	74	428	645	47,8	8,8	3,1	9	gen

(ex Guy Chipperfield-82)
Whiting Shipping Ltd

BRENDONIAN	66	604	837	54,0	9,1	3,6	10	gen

(ex Brendonia-84)
Note. Flag - (h) - Honduras   (j) - St Vincent & the Grenadines

REMA bound for Grove Wharf on the River Trent   *(David H. Smith)*

BRENDONIAN leaving Cowes

(Brian Ralfs)

HAY & CO (LERWICK) LTD.

66 Commercial Street, Lerwick, Shetland, ZE1 0NJ(01595 2533/fax 01595 2781 Telex 75295haylwk)

Managers for:
  John Fleming & Co Ltd

SHETLAND TRADER	72	798	1133	60,9	10,2	3,9	12	gen(36c)

  (ex Parkesgate-79)

PETER M. HERBERT

Bideford, N. Devon

JOHN ADAMS	34	94	165	26,0	6,0	2,8	7	gen

Note. Laid up

HOLYHEAD TOWING CO LTD.

Newry Beach Yard, Holyhead, Gwynedd, LL65 1YB (01407 760111/fax 01407 764531 Telex 61179saltow)

YEOMAN ROSE	75	499	965	42,5	10,0	3,6	9	gen bge

  (ex Island Swift-90, Seaborne Trader-87)

HUELIN-RENOUF SHIPPING SERVICES

PO Box 17, New North Quay, St Helier, Jersey, CI (01534 37401/fax 01534 26059 Telex 4192294marine)

Managers for:
  Aubreyville Ltd

HUELIN DISPATCH	71	589	1533	79,1	11,1	4,1	12	gen(77c)

  (ex Island Commodore-90)

Note. Bahamas flag

INTERNATIONAL CHARTERING PLC

15 Gloster Road, Martlesham Heath, Ipswich, Suffolk, IP5 7RJ
(01473 626646/fax 01473 610256 Telex 988832intchr)

SWIFT TRADER	77	1073	2580	79,8	13,0	5,2	12	gen

(ex Swift-85)
Note. IoM flag

INTRADA CHARTERING LTD.

75 Main Road, Gidea Park, Romford, Essex (01708 739-353/fax 01708 739-252 Telex 888793asocia)

Managers for the following vessels on charter to Scot Line Ltd:

Wolfgang & Carsten Kleige

CHARLOTTE *(a)*	69	1440	1477	77,2	11,8	4,0	11	gen(72c)

(ex Hinrich Behrmann-89, Tweed-70, Launched as Hinrich Behrmann)

E. & E. Reederei GmbH & Co m.s. "Espenis" KG

ESPE *(s)*	80	1649	1679	75,0	13,0	4,0	11	gen(118c)

(ex Espenis-81)

Reederei m.s. "Hohebank" Rass Schiffarht GmbH & Co

HOHEBANK *(b)*	78	1687	1600	79,7	12,8	3,5	11	gen(82c)

Rederij Isabel B.V.

ISABEL *(d)*	72	1472	2159	71,3	11,6	5,0	12	gen

K/S Mathilde

MATHILDE *(n)*	71	2363	2400	92,8	13,4	4,9	14	gen(178c)

(ex Anden-88, Traverway Spirit-86, Masa-86, Tainio-84, Anna Knuppel-81)

Walter Meyer

SCOT TRADER *(s)*	86	1584	1900	82,0	11,5	3,7	10	gen

(ex Wotan-93, Scot Trader-91, Wotan-86)
Note. Flag - (a) - Antigua & Barbuda (b) - Bahamas (d) - Netherlands (n) - Norway (NIS) (s) - Germany

IRISH CONTINENTAL GROUP PLC (IRISH FERRIES)

2-4 Merrion Row, Dublin 2, Irish Republic (1 6610714/fax 1 6610743 Telex 93705ifd)

Chartered tonnage:

Partenreederei m.s. "Francop" Gerd Bartels KG

EMMA	91	3818	4660	103,5	16,2	6,1	14	gen(372c)

(ex Rhein Lagan-94, Manchester Trader-92, Francop-91)

Hans-Peter Eckhoff

PHILIPP	78	2567	2937	88,4	15,5	4,9	14	gen(208c)

(ex Karat-94, Rhein Lagan-94, Isle de France-93, Karat-82, Magnolia-78 Launched as Karat)

Nautrade Inc

HORNBURG	74	989	2340	76,7	13,2	5,2	13	gen(178c)

(ex Husum-85)
Note. All Antigua & Barbuda flag see also DUNDALK SHIPOWNERS

ISLE OF MAN STEAM PACKET CO LTD.

Imperial Buildings, PO Box 5, Bath Place, Douglas, IoM, IM99 1AE
(01624 623344/fax01624 661065 Telex 629414iomspc)

PEVERIL	71	5254	1685	106,3	16,0	5,0	14	ro

(ex N. F. Jaguar-82, Penda-80, ASD Meteor-75, Holmia-73)

BELARD	79	5801	3480	105,6	18,8	5,0	16	ro

(ex Mercandian Carrier II-85, Carrier II-85, Mercandian Carrier II-84, Alianza-83, Mercandian Carrier II-83)
Note. Both IoM flag

ISLES OF SCILLY STEAMSHIP CO LTD.

Hugh Town, St Mary's, PO Box 10, Isles of Scilly
(01720 22357/fax 01720 22192) & Quay Street, Penzance, TR18 4BD (01736 62009 /fax 01736 51223)

GRY MARITHA	81	590	528	40,2	9,9	3,7	9	gen/pt

JEBSEN SHIP MANAGEMENT (LONDON) LTD.

Jebsen House, 53-55 High Street, Ruislip, Middx, HA4 7AZ
(01895 676341/fax 01895 675729 Telex 8950487jebred)

Managers for:

Altnamara Shipping PLC

RADNES		76	3885	6258	103,6	16,0	7,0	13	bulk

(ex Lugano-89, Radnes-84)

Barra Head Shipping Ltd

BARRA HEAD	(i)	80	4691	7106	110,6	17,6	7,0	12	gen

Geralia Shipping Co Ltd

HERNES	(c)	80	4924	7106	110,6	17,6	7,0	12	gen

(ex Rora Head-93)

RAFNES	(c)	76	3845	6258	103,6	16,0	6,9	13	bulk

(ex General Garcia-89, Rafnes-86)

RISNES	(c)	76	3890	6258	103,6	16,1	7,0	13	bulk

(ex General Luna-90, Ronnes-85)

Jebsens Thun Beltships Investments Ltd

TELNES	(p)	82	6944	10110	117,7	20,6	8,5	14	bulk
TINNES	(n)	83	6944	10110	117,7	20,6	8,5	14	bulk

(ex General Bonifacio-88, Tinnes-86)

Viscaya Shipping Inc

HUSNES	(p)	77	4907	7174	110,6	17,6	7,0	15	gen

(ex Hook Head-93, Sumburgh Head-90)

Note. Flag - (i) - Irish Rep   (c) - Cyprus   (n) - Norway (NIS)   (p) - Panama

R. LAPTHORN & CO LTD.

Buttercrock Wharf, Vicarage Lane, Hoo, Rochester, Kent, ME3 9LQ
(01634   250369/fax 01634 250759 Telex 96350laphoo)

ANNA MERYL	91	999	1700	69,1	9,9	3,9	9	gen

(ex Anna Maria-94)

HOOCREEK	82	498	1236	50,0	9,4	4,1	8	gen
HOOCREST	86	794	1400	58,3	9,6	3,9	9	gen
HOOPRIDE	84	794	1394	58,3	9,5	3,9	8	gen

Managers for:

Harris & Dixon (Shipbrokers) Ltd

DOWLAIS	85	794	1394	58,3	9,4	3,9	8	gen
ILONA G	90	999	1700	69,1	10,8	3,9	10	gen

Jacobs & Partners Ltd

HOO BEECH	89	794	1399	58,3	9,5	3,7	9	gen
HOO DOLPHIN	86	794	1412	58,3	9,6	3,9	9	gen
HOO MAPLE	89	794	1400	58,3	9,5	3,9	9	gen
HOO MARLIN	86	794	1400	58,3	9,5	3,9	8	gen
HOO ROBIN	89	794	1377	58,3	9,5	3,9	9	gen

Jacobs & Partners & R. Lapthorn & Co Ltd

HOO FINCH	89	794	1377	58,3	9,5	3,9	9	gen
HOO KESTREL	93	1382	2225	77,8	11,1	4,0	10	gen
HOO SWAN	86	794	1412	58,3	9,5	3,9	8	gen
HOO SWIFT	89	794	1377	58,3	9,5	3,9	9	gen

NORTHERN STAR approaching the locks at Eastham at the entrance to Manchester Ship Canal

(Mike Tomlinson)

REEDNESS passes the village of Reedness as she heads down the River Ouse

(David H. Smith)

The Cardiff-owned **CELTIC NAVIGATOR** approaches her "home" port

(Bernard McCall, courtesy of ABP Cardiff)

SILVER RIVER arrives at Glasson Dock to load for her home port of Ramsey, Isle of Man

(Bernard McCall)

HELEEN C passes Northfleet on her way up the River Thames

(Ian Willett)

OTTO BECKER heads for Avonmouth with containers from Waterford

(Bernard McCall)

The late afternoon winter sun catches the **STOLT PUFFIN** as she approaches her berth at Le Havre   *(Bernard McCall)*

Functional though unattractive, **THOMAS WEHR** leaves Le Havre for Portsmouth   *(Bernard McCall)*

HOO SWAN inward bound to Sutton Bridge on the River Nene   *(Richard Potter)*

John I. Jacobs PLC

HOO FALCON	91	1382	2225	77,8	11,1	4,0	9	gen
HOO LARCH	92	1382	2225	77,8	11,1	4,0	10	gen
HOO LAUREL	84	794	1394	58,3	9,5	3,9	8	gen
HOO PLOVER	83	499	1234	50,0	9,5	4,0	8	gen
HOO TERN	85	794	1394	58,3	9,5	3,9	8	gen
HOO WILLOW	84	499	1234	50,0	9,5	4,0	8	gen

R. A. Lapthorn Co Ltd

HOO VENTURE	82	498	1180	50,0	9,5	4,0	8	gen

John H. Whitaker (Holdings) Ltd & Bayford & Co Ltd

BETTY-JEAN	85	794	1360	58,3	9,5	3,9	8	gen
FAST KEN	92	1382	2220	77,8	11,1	4,0	9	gen

(ex Bowcliffe-94)

FREDERICK CHARLES LARKHAM & SONS LTD

Severn Mill, The Strand, Westbury-on-Severn, Glos, GL14 1PG (0452 760368/fax 0452 760368)

BACCARAT	59	293	325	45,7	8,7	2,2	8	tk bge/gen
BOXER	65	197	315	35,1	7,6	2,0	8	gen bge

WALTHER LASS

Grosse Elbstrasse 36, Hamburg-Altona, 22767, Hamburg, Germany
(040 3196088 /fax 040 3196956 Telex 2133311lass)

Agents only for:
  Northumbria Shipping Ltd

NORTHUMBRIA LASS	68	498	895	59,1	9,9	3,6	11	gen

  (ex Mary H-89, Northumbria Lass-87, Fencer Hill-79, Stevnsnaes-77)
Note. Honduras flag

BETTY-JEAN anchored off Whitstable

(Richard H. Myers)

LEAFE & HAWKES LTD.

Merrick Street, Hedon Road, Hull, HU9 1NF (01482 25951/fax 01482 225406 Telex 592654)

Managers for:

Hammann & Prahm Reedereiges mbH & Co. KG m.s. "Eric Hammann"

ERIC HAMMANN	91	1156	1323	58,8	11,7	3,6	9	gen(50c)

Hammann & Prahm Bereererungsges. mbH & Co KG m.s. "Martha Hammann"

MARTHA HAMMANN	85	1832	2287	80,7	12,7	4,2	11	gen(110c)

Hammann & Prahm GmbH & Co.KG

LORE PRAHM	89	1156	1323	58,0	11,8	3,6	9	gen(50c)
WALTER HAMMANN	88	1156	1323	58,6	11,7	3,5	9	gen(50c)

Hammann & Prahm Reederei GmbH & Co. KG m.s. "Heyo Prahm"

HEYO PRAHM	87	1156	1323	58,0	11,7	3,5	10	gen(50c)

Hammann & Prahm Bereederungsges.mbH & Co.KG m.s. "Kathe Prahm"

KATHE PRAHM	85	1720	1710	81,1	12,7	3,5	10	gen(112c)

Hammann & Prahm Reedereiges mbH & Co. m.s. "Selene Prahm"

SELENE PRAHM	94	1600	2400	75,1	12,7	4,5	10	gen
REBECCA HAMMANN	95	1600	2400	75,1	12,7	4,5	10	gen

Note. All Germany flag

LIBRA SHIPPING B.V.

Maaskade 159A, 3071 NR Rotterdam, Netherlands (010 4117740/fax 010 4117769 Telex 27439libr)

Agents only for:

Primula Ltd

BLACKBIRD	67	935	1735	75,8	11,2	4,4	12	gen

(ex Hawthorn-92, Francinaplein-77, Hunnau-73, Ortrud Muller-69)

Note. St Vincent & the Grenadines flag

KATHE PRAHM inward bound in the River Trent   *(David H. Smith)*

LOGANTOR LTD., trading as MERSEY TANKER LIGHTERAGE

17 Owarside Drive, Wallasey, Wirral, Merseyside L45 5HZ (0151 638 3813)

SAFE HAND	50	205	203	30,6	7,0	2,4	8	tk bge
(ex Lux-75)								

LOTHIAN REGIONAL COUNCIL

Edinburgh Sewage Works, 4 Marine Esplanade, Edinburgh, EH6 7LU (0131 553-1171/fax 0131 553-5804)

GARDYLOO	76	1876	2695	85,9	14,2	4,7	12	sludge

LOTHIAN SHIPPING LTD.

Jebsen House, 53-55 High Street, Ruislip, Middx, HA4 7BD
(01895 676341 /fax 01895 675729 Telex 8950487jebred)

Managers for:
  Bishopsgate Colliers Ltd

LORD CITRINE	86	14201	22447	154,9	24,5	9,0	12	bulk
LORD HINTON	86	14201	22447	154,9	24,5	9,0	12	bulk
SIR CHARLES								
PARSONS	85	14201	22447	154,9	24,5	9,0	12	bulk

THE MAERSK CO LTD.

10 Cabot Square, Canary Wharf, London, E14 4QL (0171   712-5029/fax 0171 712-5050 Telex 8812666)

Managers for :
  Norfolk Line B.V.

MAERSK FLANDERS	78	7199	3523	122,9	21,0	4,8	16	ro
(ex Duke of Flanders-90, Romira-86, Admiral Atlantic-84)								

Note. Netherlands flag

MAERSK CO (I.O.M.) LTD.

Portland House, Station Road, Ballasalla, IoM (01624 822667/fax 01624 822618 Telex 8811391)

Managers for:
Lunar Finance Ltd

MAERSK ANGLIA	77	6862	3526	122,9	21,0	4,8	15		ro

(ex Duke of Anglia-90, Saint Remy-86, Admiral Caribe-82, Admiral Nigeria-79, Admiral Caribe-77)

Note. IoM flag

MARIMED AGENCIES (UK) LTD.

27 Fishers Lane, London, W4 1RX (0181 742-3535/fax 0181 742-3394 Telex 297933marime)

Managers for :
Ballard Maritime Inc

ANAIS	85	3402	3068	93,8	16,3	6,0	14	ref(164c)

(ex Jokulfell-93)

Note. Bahamas flag

MARINE MANAGEMENT SERVICES LTD.

Eaglehurst, Belmont Hill, Douglas, IoM, IM1 4NY (01624 688886/fax 01624 688899 Telex 627564mmsiom)

Managers for:
Belfast Freight Ferries Ltd

RIVER LUNE *(b)*	83	7765	5000	121,5	21,0	5,3	15	ro(450c)

(ex Stena Topper-93, Salar-93, Stena Topper-89, Bazias 7-89, Balder Vik-86)

SPHEROID *(o)*	71	7171	2838	124,2	19,0	5,0	19	ro

(ex Niekerk-87, RoRo Trader-85, Starmark-81)

D.U.K. Shipping Ltd

NORTHERN STAR	80	1114	719	64,5	10,3	3,5	11	lpg(ch)

Note. Flag - (b) - Bahamas (o) - IoM

SPHEROID at Heysham

(Iain McCall)

MAROLINE LTD.

Alexandra Road, North Wall, Dublin 1, Irish Rep (1 8744342/fax 1 365884)

Managers for:
Bellair Enterprises Ltd
PEARL REEFER *(p)*   69   1580   1647   82,8   11,8   4,8   14   ref
   (ex Reefer Progress-91, Reefer Dolphin-85, Frio Dolphin-85, Geleszae-69)
Willingham Ltd
DIAMOND REEFER *(b)*   80   2175   4395   103,7   16,0   6,3   16   ref(32c)
   (ex Frost Cetus-92, Frost Delphi-89, Frigo Asia-86)
Note . Flag - (p) - Panama   (b) - Bahamas

ALFRED McALPINE CONSTRUCTION LTD.

Hooton, Little Sutton, South Wirral, Cheshire (0151 328 5000)

HOUND BANK   62   103   127   29,4   5,8   1,8   10   gen bge
   (ex Spurn Bank-80, Shalfleet-76)

McKITTERICK CONTRACTS

48 Summerisland Road, Loughall, Co Armagh BT71 6NQ (018687 84670)

Stephen McKitterick
ST STEPHEN   66   645   833   56,7   10,1   3,4   10   eff tk
   (ex Kingsabbey-88, Rudi M-80, Teviot-79)

MERMAID MARINE MANAGEMENT LTD.

Walkford Lane, New Milton, Hants, BH25 6DR (01425 619262/fax 01425 619237 Telex 418479)

Managers for:
Delship Corp
ALPINE GIRL   75   3911   6418   110,0   16,6   6,9   14   ch tk
   (ex Dintel-86, Quimico Lisboa-86, launched as Chemist Lisbon)
Delship Trading Corp
ALPINE LADY   77   4009   6433   110,5   16,6   6,9   13   ch tk
   (ex Multitank Antares-88, Dommel-87, Quimico Leixoes-86)
Note. Both Bahamas flag

MEZERON LTD.

East Quay, Ramsey, IoM (01624 812302/fax 01624 81563 Telex 629250mezltd)

GREEBA RIVER   69   398   713   53,0   8,8   3,3   10   gen
   (ex Tora-88, Cynthia June-86, Arklow River-82, Apollo 1-80)
SILVER RIVER   68   277   373   44,7   7,4   2,7   10   gen
   (ex Nathurn-86, Sea Trent-82, Seacon-71)
Note. Both IoM flag

MORLINE CHARTERING

Morline House, London Road, Barking, Essex, IG11 8BB (0181 507 6000/fax 0181 507 6200 Telex 889066)
Managers for:
Ansat Shipping Inc

ALMATY	78	959	1408	72,3	11,3	3,3	10	gen
(ex Militence-93)								
ANSAT	78	959	1408	72,3	11,3	3,3	10	gen
(ex Nascence-93)								
Nard-Med Shipping Ltd								
DANA (m)	73	1510	2515	80,7	11,3	5,3	11	gen
(ex Lady Dorothy-94, Orchid Star—84, Dolomit-83)								

Note. Bahamas flag except (m) - Malta

ANSAT in the River Trent

(David H. Smith)

R. G. MULLETT

17 Granary Close, Rainham, Gillingham, Kent, (01634 371162)

ROINA	66	172	264	29,4	6,8	2,5	7	gen bge

NAVIERA QUIMICA S.A.

Calle Las Mercedes 31-33°, PO Box 105, 48930 Las Arenas, Viscaya, Spain (94 464 10 99/fax 94 464 29 58)
Managers for:
Tanis Ltd

BENCENO	77	2612	3971	101,0	14,3	6,4	15	ch tk
Titus Shipping Ltd								
ESTIRENO	77	2612	3970	101,0	14,3	6,4	15	ch tk

Note. Both IoM flag

NORD SHIP MANAGEMENT LTD.

Office No.5, Terminal Building, Kirkwall Harbour, Kirkwall, Orkney (01856 870124/fax01856 870125)

Managers for:
Hamnavoe Shipping Ltd

SANMARK *	67	439	655	52,7	8,3	3,0	9	gen

(ex Ilen-93, Patmarie-89, Sanmar-87, Union Sun-84, Andre-74)
Nord Islands Shipping Ltd

NORD STAR	78	470	727	49,3	9,0	3,2	10	gen

(ex Kava Sound-94, Ordinence-89)
Nordrey Shipping Ltd

COMMODITY	75	633	946	57,6	10,0	3,3	10	gen

*Note. * to be renamed MICHAEL ANE*

NORSE SHIPPING LTD.

27 Pier Road, St Helier, PO Box 285, Jersey, Channel Islands JE4 8TZ (contact via Seacon Ltd)

SEA HUMBER	77	1602	2139	69,0	13,5	4,5	10,5	gen

Note. Bahamas flag   Time chartered to SEACON LTD qv

NORTH SEA FERRIES LTD.

King George Dock, Hedon Road, Hull, HU9 5QA (01482 795141/fax 01482 712170 Telex 52349nsf)

Managed and Chartered tonnage:
Equipment Leasing (Properties) Ltd

NORBAY	94	17464	5600	166,8	23,9	5,8	23	ro

Norbank C.V.

NORBANK *(d)*	93	17464	6790	166,8	23,9	6,0	23	ro

Norcape Shipping B.V.

NORCAPE *(d)*	79	14087	5024	150,0	20,7	5,1	19	ro(240c)

(ex Tipperary-89, Launched as Puma)
Oy Rettig Ab

NORKING *(t)*	80	6849	7984	142,1	23,0	7,6	17	ro(514c)

(ex Bore King-91)

NORQUEEN *(t)*	80	6850	7984	142,1	23,0	7,6	17	ro(514c)

(ex Bore Queen-91)
Note. Flag - (d) - Netherlands (t) - Finland   see also P&O FERRYMASTERS

NORTH WEST WATER LTD.

Dawson House, Warrington, Cheshire, WA5 3LW (01925 234000 Telex 628642dawson)

CONSORTIUM I	72	2548	3623	100,0	14,2	5,4	13	sludge
GILBERT J. FOWLER *	71	2548	3623	100,0	14,2	5,4	12	sludge

*Note. * laid up*

NORTHWOOD (FAREHAM) LTD.

Riverside House, Upper Wharf, Fareham, Hants, PO16 0NB
(01329 235717/fax 01329 822697 Telex 86736sotex)

MEDINA RIVER	69	199	424	41,8	7,7	2,7	9	sand

(ex Colby River-91, Subro Vixen-87, Tower Marie-80)

ORKNEY LINE

Hatstone Industrial Estate, Kirkwall, KW15 1ER (01856 873658/fax 01856 873563) and *(p.t.o. next page)*

SHETLAND LINE

Garthspool, Lerwick (01595 2869/fax 01595 2234)

Chartered tonnage:
Partenreederei m.s."Euro Clipper" Trans-Baltic-Schiffahrts GmbH

EURO CLIPPER	(a)	69	1217	1975	74,5	10,8	5,1	12	gen(90c)

(ex Destel-80, Owen Kirsten-77, Destel-73)
Sophinor Shipping A/S

SOPHINOR	(n)	69	499	1479	77,9	13,0	4,0	12	gen(108c)

(ex Barbara-93, Barbara-Ann-84)

Note. Flag - (a) - Antigua & Barbuda   (n) - Norway (NIS)

ORCARGO

10A Junction Road, Kirkwall, Orkney, KW15 1LB (01856 873838/fax 01856 876521)

CONTENDER	73	2294	1357	79,0	13,3	4,2	15	ro/gen(28c)

(ex Indiana I-92, Indiana-88, Ferruccio-86, Antinea-83)

P&O EUROPEAN FERRIES (DOVER) LTD.

Channel House, Channel View Road, Dover, Kent, CT17 9TJ (01304 223216/fax 01304223223 Telex 965104)

Managers for:
Abbey National March Leasing (1) Ltd
EUROPEAN

ENDEAVOUR	78	8097	3767	117,9	20,3	5,1	18	ro

(ex European Enterprise-88)
Hamton Ltd

EUROPEAN HIGHWAY	92	22986	7550	179,7	28,3	6,3	21	ro

Sutten Ltd

EUROPEAN PATHWAY	91	22986	6584	179,7	28,3	6,3	21	ro
EUROPEAN SEAWAY	91	22986	6584	179,7	28,3	6,3	21	ro

P&O EUROPEAN FERRIES (FELIXSTOWE) LTD.

Ferry Centre, The Dock, Felixstowe, Suffolk, IP11 8TB (01394 604100/fax 01394 604203 Telex 98232)

EUROPEAN FREEWAY	78	21162	8734	184,6	25,3	6,4	17	ro(562c)

(ex Cerdic Ferry-91, Stena Transporter-86, Syria-83, Alpha Enterprise-79)

EUROPEAN TIDEWAY	77	21162	8672	184,6	25,3	6,4	18	ro(562c)

(ex Doric Ferry-91, Hellas-86, Alpha Progress-79, Stena Runner-77)
Managers for:
Abbey National March Leasing (1) Ltd

EUROPEAN TRADER	75	8007	3953	117,9	20,3	5,8	18	ro

P&O EUROPEAN FERRIES (PORTSMOUTH) LTD.

Peninsular House, Wharf Road, Portsmouth, Hants, PO2 8TA
(01705 772204/fax01705 772134 Telex 869108)

Chartered tonnage:
(Oskar Wehr KG (GmbH & Co) chartered to P&O European Ferries)
Partenreederei m.s. "Gabriele Wehr"

GABRIELE WEHR	(a)	78	7635	4322	141,3	17,4	5,2	17	ro(341c)

(ex Sari-93, Gabriele Wehr-92, Tor Anglia-85, Gabriele Wehr-82)
Partenreederei m.s. "Thomas Wehr"

THOMAS WEHR	(a)	77	7297	4322	141,3	17,4	5,2	17	ro(341c)

(ex Hornlink-94, Fuldatal-94, Santa Maria-93, Mana-93, Thomas Wehr-93, Dana Germania-86,
Tor Neerlandia-85 , Thomas Wehr-82, Wacro Express-78, Launched as Thomas Wehr)

Note. Both Antigua & Barbuda flag

P&O FERRYMASTERS LTD.

Station House, Stamford New Road, Altrincham, Cheshire, WA14 1ER
(0161 928-6333/fax 0161 926-9592 Telex 668273)

NORSKY	79	14077	5024	150,0	21,8	5,1	19	ro(240c)

(ex Norsea-86, Ibex-80)
See also NORTH SEA FERRIES
Managers for:
  Elk Leasing Co Ltd

ELK	77	14374	9700	163,6	21,7	7,3	18	ro(562c)

P&O SCOTTISH FERRIES LTD.

Jamieson's Quay, PO Box 5, Aberdeen, AB9 8DL (01224 589111/fax 01224 584378 Telex 739156)

ST ROGNVALD	70	5297	3801	103,8	18,8	5,0	16	ro

(ex Marino Torre-90, Rhone-87, Rhonetal-75, Norcape-74, launched as Rhonetal)

P&O TANKSHIPS LTD.

6th Floor, West Wing, Glen House, Stag Place, London, SW1E 5AD
(0171 828-3466/fax 0171 821-5035 Telex 8950147rowman)

Managers for:
  Antares Navichem Schiffahrtsges

ANCHORMAN	93	4842	6417	101,6	17,5	6,9	12	tk

  Nordenhamer Chemikalien und Produkten GmbH & Co m.v. "Chartsman" KG

CHARTSMAN	93	4842	6417	101,6	17,5	6,9	12	tk

  Nordenhamer Chemikalien u Produkten Transport GmbH & Co m.v. "Steersman" KG

STEERSMAN	94	4842	6397	101,6	17,5	6,9	12	tk

  Rudderman Shipping Corp

RUDDERMAN	94	4842	6397	101,6	17,5	6,9	12	tk

Note. All Liberia flag

  P&O Tankships (Gibraltar) Ltd

CABLEMAN	80	4916	8496	117,2	17,5	7,2	12	tk
EASTGATE	79	2072	3415	93,2	13,4	5,3	12	tk
GUIDESMAN	80	1405	2162	70,8	12,6	4,7	11	tk

(ex Esso Plymouth-89)

IRISHGATE	81	1599	3290	93,2	13,4	5,2	12	tk
NORTHGATE	81	2071	3290	93,2	13,4	5,2	12	tk
OARSMAN	80	1449	2547	76,1	12,5	4,9	10	tk
TANKERMAN	83	5646	10716	119,7	19,2	7,8	11	tk
TILLERMAN	75	7307	12800	142,5	17,8	8,6	12	tk
WESTGATE	79	1599	3368	93,2	13,6	5,3	12	tk

Note. All Gibraltar flag

  P&O Tankships (Hong Kong) Ltd

ASTRAMAN	73	1597	3202	87,4	13,8	5,5	13	ch tk
ECHOMAN	82	3759	6125	104,3	16,7	6,8	12	oil/ch tk
STELLAMAN	80	2804	3660	97,8	13,8	5,8	12	ch tk

(ex Navajo-94, Richard-88)
Note. All Hong Kong flag

New buildings (4)		96/97	3700

TANKERMAN passing Portishead bound for Avonmouth *(Dominic McCall)*

PANDORO LTD.

Copse Road, Fleetwood, Lancs, FY7 6HR (01253 777111/fax 01253 771043 Telex 677419pdfwdg)

BISON	75	4259	7078	140,1	19,1	4,7	18	ro(52c)
BUFFALO	75	10987	4377	141,8	19,6	5,8	18	ro(52c)
EUROPEAN CLEARWAY	76	8023	3927	117,9	20,3	5,8	18	ro
PUMA	75	4377	4035	141,8	19,4	5,8	18	ro(54c)

(ex Union Trader-80, Union Melbourne-80)

VIKING TRADER	77	3985	3775	137,3	18,1	5,7	18	ro(200c)

(ex Oyster Bay-83, Manaure VII-83, Caribbean Sky-81, Federal Nova-81, Goya-79, launched as Stena Tender

See also SANDFORD SHIP MANAGEMENT

PATTERSON SHIPPING LTD.

St Peter Port, Guernsey, CI.

BORKUM II	58	497	880	55,8	9,3	3,5	10	gen

(ex AD Astra-93, Barlow-91, Oakham-91, Borkumriff-89)

Note. St Vincent & the Grenadines flag Laid up

PETROLEUM SHIPPING LTD.

Mountbatten House, Grovesnor Square, Southampton, SO15 2UX
(01703 821200/fax 01703 821390 Telex 94080840psl)

Managers for:
Esso Marine UK Ltd

PETRO AVON	81	2386	3134	91,3	13,1	5,6	12	oil/bit tk
(ex Esso Avon-94)								
PETRO CLYDE	72	11897	20776	166,5	22,9	9,2	15	tk
(ex Esso Clyde-94)								
PETRO FAWLEY	67	10631	18377	162,7	22,0	8,5	16	tk
(ex Esso Fawley-94)								
PETRO INVERNESS	71	2144	3419	91,4	12,9	5,9	13	tk
(ex Esso Inverness-94)								

PETRO MERSEY (ex Esso Mersey-94)	72	11898	20510	166,5	22,8	9,2	15	tk
PETRO MILFORD HAVEN (ex Esso Milford Haven-94)	68	10631	18377	162,7	22,0	8,5	16	tk
PETRO PENZANCE (ex Esso Penzance-94)	71	2144	3402	91,4	12,9	5,9	13	tk
PETRO SEVERN (ex Esso Severn-94)	75	11897	20776	166,5	22,9	9,2	15	tk
PETRO TYNE (ex Esso Tyne-94)	74	13340	22333	161,2	23,6	9,8	13	tk

PORT OF PEMBROKE LTD.

Sunderland House, The Old Royal Dockyard, Pembroke Dock, Dyfed, SA72 6TD
(01646 683981/fax 01646 687394 Telex 48584govan)

G . D. DISTRIBUTOR (ex Shell Distributor-91, Harty-79)	74	589	733	59,1	10,0	2,5	10	bk tk bge

PRATT ALAN J., ANNETTE, DAVID A., & MICHAEL

770 Lower Rainham Road, Rainham, Gillingham, Kent, ME8 7UB (01634 234147/fax 01634 234147)

SEVERN SIDE	52	244	406	41,0	6,5	2,5	7	gen
Managers for:								
Bartlett Creek Shipping Ltd								
LOCATOR	70	191	315	31,7	6,8	2,6	7	gen
LODELLA	70	196	315	31,7	6,8	2,6	7	gen
ROGUL	65	172	254	29,4	6,8	2,6	7	gen

J. J. PRIOR (TRANSPORT) LTD.

Ballast Quay, Fingringhoe, Essex, CO5 7DB (01206 729 412/fax 01206 729 551) and
Prior's Wharf, Canning Town, London, E16 4ST (0171 474 1677/fax 0171 474 1699)

BERT PRIOR	61	175	289	32,9	6,8	2,5	8	sand
BRENDA PRIOR (ex Cheryl M-87, Kiption-84)	68	198	279	32,3	7,0	2,7	7	sand
H. W. WILKINSON	63	187	264	30,4	6,8	2,4	8	sand
JAMES P	63	191	280	34,1	6,8	2,6	8	sand
MARK PRIOR (ex Lobe-94)	69	191	295	31,7	6,8	2,6	7	sand
PETER P (ex Fence-64, X57)	15	186	279	33,5	6,5	2,4	8	sand
Chartered Tonnage:								
Alan Jenner								
ROFFEN	65	172	261	29,4	7,1	2,5	7	sand

THE RAMSEY STEAMSHIP CO LTD.

13 North Quay, Douglas, IoM , IM1 4LE (01624 673557/fax 01624 620460 Telex 627279rssiom)

BEN ELLAN (ex River Tamar-90)	81	538	824	50,0	9,3	3,4	9	gen
BEN VANE (ex Bulk Moon-88, Julia S-81)	77	541	772	50,2	9,0	3,4	9	gen

RIGEL SCHIFFAHRTS GmbH

World Trade Center, Birkenstrasse 15, 28195 Bremen, Germany (0421 1691450/fax 0421 1691455)
Managers for:
Chem Carriers Ltd

WESERSTERN	92	5480	9028	109,7	17,7	8,5	12	oil/ch tk
Chemshipping Ltd								
ODERSTERN	92	5480	9028	109,7	17,7	8,5	12	oil/ch tk

Note. Both IoM flag

J. R. RIX & SONS LTD.

Witham House, 45 Spyvee Street, Hull, HU8 7JR (01482 224422 /fax 01482 227644 & 586511)

BELDALE H	59	207	320	50,9	5,2	2,3	8	tk bge
JONRIX (b)	77	999	2210	79,0	12,5	4,8	11	gen(104c)
(ex Langeland II-94, Langeland-83)								
RIX EAGLE	90	292	500	50,0	6,0	3,0	8	tk bge
RIX FALCON	60	172	250	43,3	5,4	2,1	8	tk
(ex Burtondale H-92)								
RIX KESTREL	57	206	320	50,9	5,4	2,3	8	tk bge
(ex Burdale H-93)								

Managers for:
The Magrix Shipping Co Ltd

MAGRIX	76	998	1897	78,4	10,8	4,1	11	gen

(ex The Dutch-87, Tanja Holwerda-87, Roelof Holwerda-81)
Robrix Shipping Co Ltd

ROBRIX	75	791	1184	61,7	10,5	3,9	12	gen

(ex Silloth Stag-85, launched as Tilstone Maid)
Timrix Shipping Co Ltd

TIMRIX (b)	72	818	1393	72,7	10,5	3,8	12	gen

(ex Ellie-84, Nellie M 82)

Note. (b) - Bahamas flag

MAGRIX in Alexandra Dock, Hull   *(David H. Smith, courtesy ABP Hull)*

W. RUTLAND

Cornwall Wharf, Wharf Road, Gravesend, DA12 2RU (01474 323856/fax 01474 333391)

ROAN	61	138	250	27,7	6,5	2,5	7	gen bge

SALLY FREIGHT LTD.

Argyle House, York Street, Ramsgate, Kent, CT11 9DS (01843 595566/fax 01843 593454) and
Dartford International Freight Terminal, Dartford (01322 281122)

Managers for:
Gotland Shipping Ltd

SALLY SUN	79	6643	1950	118,5	16,9	4,0	16	ro(185c)

(ex Gute-92)
International Trailer Service

SALLY EUROBRIDGE	77	1598	3046	116,3	18,2	5,4	15	ro(140c)

(ex Eurobridge-94, Sally Eurobridge-94, Schiaffino-93, Tikal-89, Haila-88, Mashala-86)
Rosal S. A.

SALLY EUROLINK	85	2831	4700	120,0	21,0	5,3	14	ro(450c)

(ex Bazias 4-93, Balder Bre-85)

SALLY EUROROUTE	84	2831	4700	120,0	21,0	5,3	14	ro(450c)

(ex Bazias 3-93, Balder Sten-85)
Chartered tonnage:
SALLY EUROWAY *(s)* From April '95 - details to be announced
Note. All Bahamas flag except (s) - Germany

SANDFORD SHIP MANAGEMENT LTD.

Neptune House, Sandford, Ventnor, IoW, PO38 3AN (01983 840133/fax 01983 840190 Telex 86410)

Managers for:
Marine Atlantic Inc chartered to Pandoro Ltd, Fleetwood
ATLANTIC

FREIGHTER	78	5465	8661	151,0	21,7	7,3	16	ro(562c)

(ex Stena Grecia-86, Merzario Grecia-83, Tor Felicia-78)
Marine Atlantic Inc chartered to Meridian Ferries Ltd, Folkestone

SPIRIT OF BOULOGNE	74	2793	1856	110,1	17,5	5,8	18	ro

(ex Marine Evangeline-93, Duke of Yorkshire-78)
Caribia Ferries S.A. chartered to Meridian Ferries Ltd, Folkestone
SPIRIT OF

INDEPENDENCE	69	4623	772	118,2	17,8	4,4	22	ro/pass *

(ex Caribia Viva-94, Sardinia Viva-93, Corsica Viva-92, Dominican Viva-88, Corsica Viva-85, Innisfallen-80)
*Note. All Bahamas flag * trading freight only*

SEACON LTD.

The London Steel Terminal, Express Wharf, 38 West Ferry Road, London, E14 8LW
(0171 987-1291/fax 0171 987-2915 Telex 897181 seacon)

Chartered tonnage:
Briese Schiffahrts GmbH & Co KG m.s. "Sea Danube"

SEA DANUBE *(a)*	88	910	994	69,1	9,5	2,8	10	gen(36c)

Briese & Buss Schiffahrts GmbH & Co KG m.s. "Leda"

SEA DOURO *(a)*	88	910	1085	69,1	9,5	3,0	10	gen(36c)

(launched as Leda)
Briese Schiffahrts GmbH & Co KG "Hamburger Sand"

SEA EMS *(s)*	84	1410	1562	79,0	10,9	3,3	10	gen(80c)

Gerhard Ahrens KG Reederei m.s. "Magula"

SEA MAGULA *(s)*	80	1655	1548	83,0	11,4	3,2	11	gen(72c)

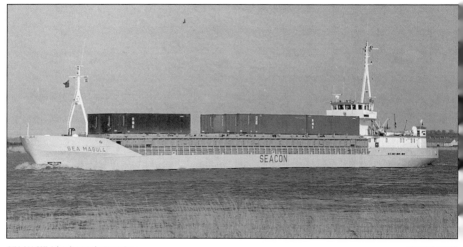

SEA MAGULA heading up the River Ouse   (David H. Smith)

Medrhone Shipping Ltd
| SEA RHONE | (v) | 94 | 1525 | 2000 | 81,6 | 11,3 | 3,7 | 10 | gen |

Natissa Shipping Ltd
| SEA RUHR | (v) | 95 | 1525 | 2000 | 81,6 | 11,3 | 3,7 | 10 | gen |

Reederei Frank Dahl m.s. "Merlan"
| SEA MERLAN | (s) | 78 | 1495 | 1550 | 76,8 | 11,5 | 3,4 | 11 | gen(62c) |

(launched as Merlan)
Partenreederei m.s. "Mosel"
| SEA MOSEL | (a) | 79 | 1456 | 1703 | 81,9 | 10,0 | 3,6 | 10 | gen |

(ex Huberna-89)
Reederei Frank Dahl m.s. "Orade" KG
| SEA ORADE | (s) | 90 | 1354 | 1699 | 77,0 | 11,4 | 3,2 | 10 | gen(94c) |

(launched as Orade)
Reederei m.s. "Neckar"
| SEA THAMES | (a) | 85 | 1616 | 1922 | 82,5 | 11,4 | 3,8 | 10 | gen(67c) |

(ex Kurt Jensen-94)
Josef Gerdes Schiffahrtsges mbH & Co KG m.s. "Sea Trent"
| SEA TRENT | (a) | 84 | 1289 | 1558 | 74,9 | 10,6 | 3,4 | 10 | gen |

(ex Echo Venture-90, Sea Trent-90)
Note. Flag - (a) - Antigua & Barbuda (s) - Germany (v) - Luxembourg; see also AGRI-TRANS ,
DUNDALK SHIPOWNERS & NORSE SHIPPING

SEASCOT SHIPMANAGEMENT LTD.
45 Carrick Street, Glasgow, G2 8PJ (0141 226-3733/fax 0141 204-3276Telex 776618seascot)
Managers for:
Gallic Shipping Ltd
| GAUSS F | (e) | 77 | 1591 | 3256 | 91,5 | 13,3 | 5,1 | 12 | gen(60c) |

(ex Gallic Fjord-93)
North Bay Shipping Ltd
| LESZEK G | (q) | 77 | 1592 | 3256 | 91,5 | 13,3 | 5,2 | 12 | gen(60c) |

(ex Leslie Gault-92)
Seascot Shiptrading Ltd
| MALIN SEA | (e) | 73 | 1599 | 3776 | 84,3 | 14,4 | 6,3 | 14 | gen |

(ex Marijke-91, Marijke Smits-83)
Note. Flag - (e) - Vanuatu   (q) - Poland

SEAWARD ENGINEERING

974 Pollokshaws Road, Glasgow, G41 2HA (0141 632 4910 /fax 0141 636 1194)

SULBY RIVER	71	196	269	30,6	7,1	2,4	8	gen

(ex Subro Venture-84)
Note. IoM flag - Laid up repairing

SEAWAY S.A.M.

20 boulevard de Suisse, 98000 Monte Carlo, Monaco (25.13.92/fax 15.09.52 Telex 469488marsud)

Managers for:
  Protac Shipping Ltd

MEDUNION	80	1082	1579	70,0	11,3	3,6	11	gen

(ex Union Arrow-92)
Note. Gibraltar flag

SOENDERBORG REDERIAKTIESELSKAB (SONDERBORG STEAMSHIP CO LTD.)

Havnevej 18, PO Box 20, 6320 Egernsund, Denmark (74 441435/fax 74 441475 Telex 52815sra)

Managers for:
  Clovis Navigation S.A.
  GERARD PATRICK

PURCELL *(p)*	70	2978	2568	88,5	13,9	5,5	13	l/v

(ex Deichtor-83, Lubbecke-83, Ibesca Belgica-80, Ibesca Britannia-78, Lubbecke-77)
  K/S Philomena
  PHILOMENA

PURCELL *(n)*	73	1236	2650	88,3	13,0	5,0	13	l/v

(ex Esteflut-82)
Note. Flag - (n) - Norway (NIS) (p) - Panama

SHELL U. K. LTD.

Room 789, Shell-Mex House, Strand, PO Box 148, London, WC2R 0DX
(0171 257-3000/fax 0171 257-3440 Telex 22585shell)

ACHATINA	68	1580	2654	84,3	12,5	4,7	14	tk

(ex Shell Craftsman-93, Ardrossan-79)

AMORIA	81	1926	3027	79,3	13,2	5,5	12	tk

(ex Shell Marketer-93)

ARIANTA	82	1926	3027	79,3	13,2	5,5	12	tk

(ex Shell Technician-93)

ASPRELLA	81	1926	3027	79,2	13,2	5,5	12	tk

(ex Shell Seafarer-93)
Time Chartered:
  Shell Nederland Raffinaderij B.V.

ACILA *(d)*	82	8806	11548	140,8	21,2	7,3	14	tk

(ex Shelltrans-94)
Note. (d) - Netherlands flag

SLOMAN NEPTUN SCHIFFAHRTS - AKTIENGESELLSCHAFT

Langenstrasse 52-54, Postfach 101469, 28195 Bremen, Germany
(0421 17630/fax 0421 1763313 Telex 244421snbr)

Managers for:
Deltagas Shipping Co Ltd

DELTAGAS	92	3011	3525	88,4	14,2	6,2	14	lpg
Gammagas Shipping Co Ltd								
GAMMAGAS	92	3703	4437	99,4	15,0	6,5	14	lpg

Note. Both Liberia flag

SMALL & CO (SHIPPING) LTD.

Waveney Chambers, Waveney Road, Lowestoft, Suffolk, NR32 1BP (01502 572301/fax 01502 515915)

| CRASKE | 28 | 83 | 128 | 24,8 | 4,4 | 2,3 | 7 | bk tk bge |

(ex Waterboat No 9-82, Veracitie-49, Severn Venturer)

SOUTH WEST WATER PLC

Exewater, Eagle Way, Exeter, Devon, EX2 7HY (01392 445544/fax 01392 444694)

| COUNTESS WEAR | 63 | 256 | 366 | 37,5 | 7,5 | 3,1 | 8 | sludge |

(ex S.W.2-75)

ST HELIER PORT SERVICES LTD.

New North Quay, St Helier, Jersey, Channel Islands, (01534 70300/fax 01534 30234)

Managers for:
E.C.C. Construction Materials Ltd

| RONEZ | 82 | 837 | 1117 | 64,7 | 10,1 | 3,5 | 10 | cem |

RONEZ leaving Le Havre

(Barry Standerline)

STEPHENSON CLARKE SHIPPING LTD.

Eldon Court, Percy Street, Newcastle upon Tyne, NE99 1TD
(0191 232-2184/fax 0191 261-1156 Telex 53696scsncl)

ALDRINGTON	(o)	78	4297	6570	103,6	16,1	7,0	14	gen
AMETHYST		87	8254	11901	142,9	20,1	7,2	12	bulk
(ex Cardona-93)									
ASHINGTON	(o)	79	4297	6570	103,6	16,1	7,0	14	gen
BIRLING	(o)	77	2795	4300	91,3	14,6	5,5	14	gen
DURRINGTON	(o)	81	7788	11990	137,6	18,7	7,9	14	gen
EMERALD	(o)	78	2795	4300	91,3	14,6	5,5	14	gen
GEM		74	7482	11848	135,7	19,3	8,3	12	bulk
(ex Guardo-92)									
HARTING	(o)	81	2813	4300	91,3	14,6	5,8	12	gen(32c)
STEYNING	(o)	83	2808	4300	91,3	14,6	5,8	12	gen(32c)
STORRINGTON	(o)	82	7788	11990	137,6	18,7	7,9	14	gen
New building	mid 96		15000	141,4	22,5	8,3	13		bulk

Managers for:
Joint Lease Ltd

JEVINGTON		77	7702	12328	127,4	19,5	8,1	13	bulk
(ex Elizabete-89, Garrison Point-88)									

M. H. Shipping Co Ltd

DALLINGTON		75	7788	12140	137,6	18,7	7,9	14	gen
DONNINGTON		75	7788	12140	137,6	18,7	7,9	14	gen

Mobil Shipping Co Ltd

LUBCHEM		73	1999	3310	93,3	14,0	5,4	12	ch tk
(ex Mobil Lubchem-91)									

Time chartered:
James Fisher & Sons PLC *

LANCING		76	1943	3109	83,5	14,1	5,2	12	gen
(ex Ballykern-90, Baxtergate-80)									
WORTHING		75	1938	3000	83,5	14,1	5,1	12	gen
(ex Ballykelly-90, Lis Danielsen-79)									

Lexham Shipping Ltd

HARRIET	(m)	71	1514	3220	87,0	12,7	5,0	12	gen
(ex Beeding-90)									

Stephenson Clarke Shipping Ltd, demise chartered to **Point Shipping Co**, Dundalk

DUNANY	(i)	83	1785	2535	77,1	13,2	5,0	12	gen
(ex Cowdray-94, Ballygrainey-90)									
HOPE	(i)	82	1599	2535	77,1	13,2	5,0	12	gen
(ex Shoreham-93, Ballygarvey-90)									

Stephenson Clarke Shipping Ltd, demise chartered to **Losinjska Plovibda Brodarstvo**, Mali Losinj

WASHINGTON	(k)	77	6400	9008	127,0	18,7	7,6	14	gen

*Note. Flag - (i) - Irish (o) - IoM (k) - Croatia (m) - Malta * technical managers Coe Metcalf Shpg*

STOLT-NIELSEN SHIPPING LTD.

Aldwych House, 71-91 Aldwych, London, WC2B 4HN (071 404 4455/fax 071 831 3100)

Commercial operators for;
Stolt Avocet Inc

STOLT AVOCET	92	3853	5749	99,9	16,8	6,8	12	ch tk

Stolt Colina Inc

STOLT COLINA	76	1592	3455	96,0	14,1	5,5	13	ch tk
(ex La Colina-89)								

Stolt Egret Inc

STOLT EGRET	92	3853	5758	99,9	17,1	6,8	12	ch tk

WASHINGTON at Londonderry   *(Alan Geddes)*

Stolt Kestrel Inc								
STOLT KESTREL	92	3853	5741	99,9	17,1	6,8	12	ch tk
STOLT PUFFIN	92	3853	5758	99,9	17,1	6,8	12	ch tk
Stolt Maplewood Inc								
STOLT MAPLEWOOD	76	2564	3560	89,2	14,0	5,9	13	ch tk
(ex Maplewood-89, Centaurman-87)								
Stolt Oakwood Inc								
STOLT OAKWOOD	76	2564	3560	89,2	14,1	5,9	13	ch tk
(ex Oakwood-89, Vegaman-87, Essex Triumph-83, Vegaman-83)								
Stolt Pradera Inc								
STOLT PRADERA	76	1592	3455	96,0	14,1	5,5	13	ch tk
(ex La Pradera-89)								
Stolt Trusty Inc								
KINGFISHER *(l)*	86	1963	3283	88,0	13,6	5,5	12	ch tk
(ex Stolt Kingfisher-94, Trusty-88)								

Time charter:
  K/S Ringkobing VI (Terkildsen & Olsen A/S) chartered by Stolt Nielsen Shipping Ltd

ELLA TERKOL *(w)*	90	1711	3294	83,5	13,7	5,5	10	ch tk

Note. All Norway (NIS) flag except (l) - Liberia (w) - Denmark

STRATHCLYDE REGIONAL COUNCIL
(Dept of Sewerage),   Strathclyde House, 20 India Street, Glasgow, G2 4PF
(0141 204-2900/fax 0141 227-2870 Telex 777237srchq)

DALMARNOCK	70	2266	3266	95,4	15,6	4,4	12	sludge
GARROCH HEAD	77	2808	3671	98,7	16,0	4,4	11	sludge

SWINSHIP MANAGEMENT B.V.

Ringdijk 516, 2987 VZ Ridderkerk, Netherlands
(01804 19248 & 18414/fax 01804 11341 Telex 28166swins)

Managers for:
Onesimus Dorey (Shipowners) Ltd chartered to Swinship Management

TEAL I	74	945	1447	60,9	9,8	4,3	11	gen

(ex Hoxa Sound-94, Murell-88)
Onesimus Dorey (Shipowners) Ltd/Wardwood Chartering Ltd

ALBATROSS I	79	1159	1690	68,0	11,8	4,3	11	gen

(ex Janet C-93, Fastnet Rock-90)

CORMORANT I	74	992	1643	67,7	11,8	4,0	11	gen

(ex Betty C-93, Kerry M-87, Sentence-85)

SEA EAGLE I	78	1159	1690	68,0	11,8	4,3	11	gen

(ex Eileen C-93, Tuskar Rock-90)
Note. All St Vincent & the Grenadines flag

W. D. TAMLYN & CO LTD.

Victoria Wharf, Plymouth, Devon, PL4 0RF
(01752 663444/fax 01752 221979 Telex 45247 tamlyn g)

Managers for:
Bay of Bouley Ltd

ALICE *(b)*	82	998	1688	67,4	11,3	4,1	10	gen(54c)

(ex Alila-92, Peacock Venture-88)
Cornish Shipping (C.I.) Ltd

VENDOME *(g)*	79	487	878	48,8	9,1	3,8	10	gen

(ex Peroto-94)
Naviera Cuyamel S.A.

VAUBAN *(h)*	71	696	1013	63,5	10,0	3,7	12	gen

(ex Vasa Sound-94, Paquita-93, Clafen-83, Fendyke-82)
Note. Flag - (b) - Bahamas (g) - Gibraltar (h) - Honduras

TORBULK LTD.

The Old Rectory, Bargate, Grimsby, Sth Humberside, DN34 4SY
(01472 242363/fax 01472 242329 Telex 378525torblk)

Managers for:
Cove Shipping Co Ltd

FOSSELAND *(b)*	79	1059	1559	66,9	10,8	4,1	11	gen(58c)

(ex Perelle-94)

RUTLAND *(b)*	75	1594	2583	77,8	13,2	5,0	13	gen

(ex Martindyke-88)

NANCY *(p)*	77	1576	3200	81,0	13,5	5,4	12	gen

(ex Blue Dream-94, Depatre-91, Centotre-88)
Note. Flag - (p) - Panama (b) - Bahamas ; see also Onesimus Dorey (Shipowners) Ltd under
F. T. EVERARD

TYNE WATER BOATS LTD.

29 Laburnum Grove, Cleadon, Sunderland, Tyne & Wear, SR6 7RJ
(0191 536 2335, 0191 455 2427 & 0860 899928)

ABERCRAIG	45	138	180	31,7	6,0	2,2	7	wt tk bge

(ex Ernie Spearing-74, Attunity-67, MOB 9-52)

HARCUSS	32	96	150	26,5	5,2	2,7	7	wt tk bge

U.B. SHIPPING LTD.

3rd Floor, 2/4 Great Eastern Street, London, EC2A 3NT
(0171 247-3377/fax 0171 247-4192 Telex 919912ubline)

SAFIYE SULTAN	71	375	818	57,8	10,3	3,5	12	ref

(ex Minireefer-86, African Trader I-85, Svanur-82, Sofia Lasson-73)

UB PIONEER	77	1599	4150	93,3	13,8	6,0	12	gen(122c)

(ex Polly Pioneer-92,Midia-88, Gulf Empress-85, Mercandian Star-82)

UB PREMIER	75	1599	4215	89,7	13,6	6,0	14	gen(122c)

(ex Polly Premier-92, Agnes Dania-85)

UB PRESTIGE	77	1599	4135	93,3	13,8	6,0	12	gen(122c)

(ex Polly Prestige-92, Antigoni-88, Gulf Duchess-85, Mercandian Moon-82)

UB PROGRESS	70	1506	2873	87,0	15,0	6,2	15	ro/gen

(ex Polly Progress-92, Skafta-86, Borre-81)

UB PROSPER	75	1600	4148	89,7	13,6	6,0	13	gen

(ex Polly Prosper-92, Flamal-88, Rosa Dania-83)

Note. All Bahamas flag
Managers for:
K/S Geranta

UB PANTHER	77	3622	4415	97,5	16,1	5,7	14	gen(343c)

(ex Geranta-94, Gracechurch Star-91, Geranta-89, Karen Oltmann-89, Neerlandia-85, Karen Oltmann-78)
K/S Gerina

GERINA	73	2130	2532	81,4	13,4	4,9	14	gen(165c)

(ex Rendsburg-90, Anna Becker-84, Killarney-79, Anna Becker-77, Scol Enterprise-77, lchd as Anna Becker)
K/S Gerland

TEUTONIA	72	2441	2685	92,1	13,1	4,7	13	gen(180c)

(ex Ocean Pride-88, Teutonia-87)
K/S Gerlena

GERLENA	74	2130	2503	81,4	13,4	4,9	13	gen(165c)

(ex Achat-89, Osteland-82, Nic Trader-79, Osteland-79, Thunar-76, Osteland-74)
K/S Gerlin

GERLIN	77	2282	2560	81,4	13,4	5,0	13	gen(150c)

(ex Susan Borchard-91, Orion-90)
K/S Iberia

DUKE	77	2282	2560	81,4	13,4	5,0	13	gen(174c)

(ex Dana Iberia-91, Commodore Clipper-90, Hamburg-88, Jan Kahrs-86)
Note. All Norway (NIS) flag

GERINA arriving at Hull

(Richard Myers, courtesy of ABP Hull)

UNION TRANSPORT GROUP PLC

Imperial House, 21-25 North Street, Bromley, BR1 1SJ
(0181 290-1234/fax 0181 464-5609 Telex 896021utrans)

UNION ARBO *(b)*	84	1522	1720	82,5	11,4	3,5	10	gen(80c)
(ex Birka-94)								
UNION JUPITER	90	2230	3274	99,7	12,6	4,3	11	gen(114c)
UNION MARS *(i)*	81	935	1448	69,9	11,3	3,3	11	gen
UNION MERCURY	91	2252	3085	81,5	14,4	5,3	12	gen
(ex Donon-93)								
UNION MOON *(i)*	85	1543	2376	87,7	11,1	3,9	10	gen(98c)
UNION NEPTUNE *(i)*	85	1543	2376	87,7	11,1	3,9	10	gen(98c)
UNION SUN *(i)*	85	1543	2376	87,7	11,1	3,9	10	gen(98c)
UNION TITAN *(i)*	86	1543	2376	87,7	11,1	3,9	10	gen(98c)
UNION TOPAZ	85	1543	2362	87,7	11,1	3,9	10	gen(98c)
(ex Bromley Topaz-92, Union Topaz-90)								
Managers for:								
Rederij H. Steenstra								
ANNE S *(d)*	86	1139	1601	79,1	10,4	3,3	11	gen(80c)
DOUWE S *(d)*	87	1311	1800	79,7	10,6	3,7	10	gen(78c)
(ex Torpe-93)								

Note. Flag - *(b)* - Bahamas *(i)* - Irish Republic *(d)* - Netherlands   see also BROMLEY SHIPPING

UNION NEPTUNE inward bound in the River Trent

(Richard Potter)

THE UNITED KINGDOM GOVERNMENT

(Dept of Environment for Northern Ireland), 1 College Square East, Belfast, BT1 6DR

DIVIS II	79	820	892	56,0	11,2	3,3	10	sludge

V. SHIPS (UK) LTD.

Price Waterhouse Building, 30, Channel Way, Ocean Village, Southampton, SO1 1TG
(01703 634477/fax 01703 634319 Telex 477501vshpuk)

Managers for:
  Proofbrand Ltd

MERCHANT BRAVERY *(b)*	78	9368	5290	134,8	21,7	6,5	17	ro(524c)
(ex Jolly Giallo-93, Norwegian Crusader-82, Jolly Giallo-82, Norwegian Crusader-80 launched as Stevi)								
MERCHANT BRILLIANT *(b)*	79	9368	5300	133,1	21,7	5,0	16	ro(524c)
(ex Jolly Bruno-93, Norwegian Challenger-82)								
MERCHANT VALIANT *(b)*	78	5897	3046	116,3	18,2	5,4	15	ro(210c)
(ex Salahala-90)								
MERCHANT VENTURE *(o)*	79	6056	3671	119,4	19,5	5,2	17	ro(169c)
(ex Merchant Isle-87, Argentea-87, Med Adriatico-85, Farman-82)								
MERCHANT VICTOR *(b)*	78	5881	3046	116,3	18,2	5,4	15	ro(210c)
(ex Emadala-90)								

Note. Flag - (b) - Bahamas   (o) - IoM

WALD & RAHM MANAGEMENT AB

PO Box 12064, 402 41 Gothenburg, Sweden

Managers for:
  Stena Carrier Ltd

STENA CARRIER	78	13117	8661	151,0	20,5	7,3	16	ro(562c)
(ex Jolly Smeraldo-83, Jolly Bruno-82, Stena Carrier-82, Imparca Miami-81, Stena Carrier-80, Imparca Express I-80)								

Note. Cayman Islands flag

THOMAS WATSON (SHIPPING) LTD.

252 High Street, Rochester, Kent, ME1 1HZ (01634 844632/4/fax 01634 831838 Telex 96109watson)

Managers for:
  Andrean Shipping Ltd

LADY ELSIE *(c)*	75	955	1593	65,8	10,5	4,3	10	gen
(ex Canvey-92, Velox-88)								
LADY REA *(c)*	78	1954	3265	81,7	14,1	5,5	12	gen
(ex Ortrud-90, Carib Sun-88, Reggeland-87, Sylvia Delta-85)								
Lakehead Shipping Ltd								
LADY JILL *(b)*	81	1510	3617	80,9	13,5	6,0	11	gen(162c)
(ex Tresmares-86)								
LADY PATRICIA *(b)*	70	1547	2538	80,8	11,3	5,3	11	gen
(ex Orchid Wave-85, Diabas-83)								
LADY SYLVIA *(b)*	79	1707	2703	73,4	13,2	5,1	11	gen
(ex Inishfree—94, Arklow Vale-88, Capricorn-85)								

Note. Flag - (c) - Cyprus   (b) - Bahamas

ANDREW WEIR SHIPPING LTD.

Dexter House, 2 Royal Mint Court, London, EC3N 4XX
(0171 265-0808/fax 0171 816-4992 Telex 887392weirco)

BALTIC EAGLE	79	14738	9450	137,1	26,0	8,2	18	ro(354c)
BALTIC EIDER	89	20865	13866	157,7	25,3	8,5	19	ro(700c)
BALTIC TERN	89	3896	3754	106,6	16,2	5,4	13	cc(316c)
CERVANTES	78	3992	4352	104,2	16,8	5,7	14	cc(300c)
(ex City of Plymouth-93)								
CITY OF								
MANCHESTER	79	3992	4352	04,2	16,8	5,7	14	cc(300c)
(ex Laxfoss-85, City of Hartlepool-84)								

Note. All IoM flag
Chartered tonnage:
    Reederei m.s. "Cimbria" Harald Winter KG

CHURRUCA *(s)*	91	3815	4654	103,5	16,2	6,1	14	gen(372c)
(ex Cimbria-93, Lloyd Iberia-92, Dana Sirena-91, launched as Cimbria)								
Sarah Shipping Co Ltd								
SARAH *(a)*	91	2705	3982	89,5	13,6	5,3	12	gen(218c)

Note. Flag - (a) - Antigua & Barbuda (s) - Germany

THE WHITAKER GROUP

Crown Dry Dock, Tower Street, Hull, HU9 1TY (01482 20444/fax 01482 214850 Telex 597632bargit & 527632bargit) John H. Whitaker (Tankers) Ltd - Southern Division - Ocean Road Eastern Docks, Southampton, SO1 1AH (01703 339989/fax 01703 339925 Telex 47172 bargit)

John H. Whitaker (Holdings) Ltd

WHITONIA	83	498	1180	50,0	9,5	4,0	9	gen

John H. Whitaker (Tankers) Ltd

WHITASK	78	640	844	57,3	10,9	2,9	10	tk
(ex Bromley-93)								
WHITCREST	70	2144	3430	91,3	13,1	5,9	14	tk
(ex Esso Tenby-94)								
WHITIDE	70	1148	2083	74,5	10,2	4,9	11	tk
(ex Lindvag-90, Tarnvik-78)								
WHITSPRAY	69	899	1321	64,6	11,1	3,4	10	tk
(ex Bristolian-93)								
WHITSTAR	68	999	2140	74,3	10,2	4,8	11	tk
(ex Furena-91, Furenas-90, Stardex-79, Lone Wonsild)								

John H. Whitaker (Tankers) Ltd - Bristol Channel

WHITHAVEN	72	1210	1933	66,2	11,5	5,0	11	tk
(ex Frank C-94, Shell Director-93, Caernarvon-79)								

John H. Whitaker (Holdings) Ltd

WHITANK	76	682	1030	61,0	9,3	3,7	11	tk
(ex Luban-87)								

John H. Whitaker (Tankers) Ltd - Humber Area

DAVID W	56	213	330	47,0	5,5	2,6	7	tk bge
FARNDALE	67	293	500	55,4	5,7	2,8	8	tk bge
(ex Farndale H-89)								
FOSSDALE H	67	293	500	55,4	5,7	2,4	8	tk bge
FUSEDALE H	68	293	500	55,4	5,7	2,4	8	tk bge
HUMBER ENDEAVOUR	81	380	650	60,8	6,0	2,4	8	tk bge
(ex Fleet Endeavour-92)								
HUMBER ENERGY	83	380	650	60,8	6,0	2,4	8	tk bge
HUMBER ENTERPRISE	67	295	450	55,4	5,7	2,4	8	tk bge
HUMBER FUELLER	57	192	300	43,8	5,5	2,4	7	tk bge
HUMBER JUBILEE	77	382	650	60,9	6,0	2,7	9	tk bge
HUMBER PRIDE	79	380	650	60,8	6,0	2,4	8	tk bge
HUMBER PRINCESS	79	380	650	60,8	6,0	2,4	8	tk bge
HUMBER PROGRESS	80	380	650	60,8	6,0	2,4	8	tk bge
HUMBER RENOWN	67	295	500	55,4	5,7	2,4	8	tk bge
HUMBER STAR	69	274	400	45,7	6,6	2,2	7	tk bge
(ex Wade Stone-77)								

John Harker Ltd - Mersey Area

BAYSDALE H	60	569	950	62,7	10,4	2,8	9	tk bge
(ex Bold Knight-88)								
DEEPDALE H	65	385	580	46,2	8,3	3,4	7	tk bge
(ex Riverbeacon-67)								
DOVEDALE H	62	306	550	47,5	6,6	2,7	7	tk bge
(ex Riverbridge-67)								
WHARFDALE H	60	609	1126	61,9	8,8	3,2	8	tk bge
CLYDE ENTERPRISE	60	263	520	45,5	6,3	3,0	7	tk bge

John H.Whitaker (Tankers) Ltd - Richborough

WHITKIRK	69	730	1219	64,6	9,2	3,7	10	tk
(ex Borman-89)								

WHITSEA (ex Bude-92)	71	728	1229	64,3	9,3	3,7	10	tk

John H. Whitaker (Tankers) Ltd - Southampton Area

BATTLESTONE (ex Battlestone C- 89, Battle Stone-76)	68	293	500	55,4	5,7	2,4	9	tk bge
BORROWDALE H (ex Shell Transporter-84, Poilo-79)	72	385	550	50,6	6,7	3,1	8	tk bge
HUMBER TRANSPORTER	67	645	960	58,9	10,7	2,9	9	tk bge
SOLENT RAIDER (ex James Rayel-89, Vermion-84, Bebington-83, Pando-77)	68	605	1056	58,9	10,7	2,9	9	tk bge
TEESDALE H (ex Wilks-86)	76	499	1050	43,9	10,0	3,9	8	tk

John H. Whitaker (Tankers) Ltd - Thames/Medway

GROVEDALE (ex Grovedale H-94)	66	364	570	50,3	6,6	3,4	8	tk bge

See also R. LAPTHORN

WILLIAMS SHIPPING MARINE LTD.

Berth 21, Ocean Road, Eastern Docks, Southampton, SO14 3GF
(01703 237330/fax 01703 236151 Telex 47436 wilshp)

MURIUS	62	125	213	29,8	6,2	2,0	7	gen bge

CHARLES M. WILLIE & CO (SHIPPING) LTD.

Celtic House, Britannic Road, Roath Basin, Cardiff, CF1 5LS
(01222 471000/fax 01222 471999 Telex 498239willie)

CELTIC CHALLENGER (ex Argo Valour-86)	78	1557	3055	80,0	14,0	5,3	14	gen
CELTIC NAVIGATOR *(b)* (ex Wilant-89, Marant-88, Engel Klein-83)	79	1010	1538	65,8	11,1	4,3	10	gen
CELTIC VENTURE *(b)* (ex Norman Commodore-91)	71	1285	1533	79,0	11,1	4,1	12	gen(77c)
CELTIC VOYAGER *(b)* (ex Alannah Weston-84	75	1015	1519	65,7	10,8	4,1	10	gen
EURO MERCHANT *(b)* (ex Celtic Warrior-93)	91	3779	5878	92,8	17,1	6,6	15	gen(380c)
EURO TRADER *(b)* (ex Celtic Crusader-93)	92	3779	5878	92,8	17,1	6,6	15	gen(380c)
FAIRWAY *(b)* (ex Celtic Commander-94)	93	3840	5833	92,8	17,1	6,5	15	gen(380c)
FAIRWIND *(b)* (ex Celtic Ambassador-94)	94	3840	5833	92,8	17,1	6,5	15	gen(380c)
CELTIC PRINCE	95		6250				15	gen(467c)
CELTIC SOVEREIGN	96		6250				15	gen(467c)
New building	97		6250				15	gen(467c)
New building	97		6250				15	gen(467c)

Managers for:
Biscay Shipping Ltd

BISCAY PRIDE *(b)* (ex Izarraitz-87)	78	866	1195	62,6	10,7	4,0	12	gen
BISCAY SPIRIT *(b)* (ex Irimo-87)	78	866	1195	63,7	10,6	4,0	12	gen

Iberian Seaways (Shipping) Ltd

IBERIAN COAST (b)	79	1029	1391	72,2	11,3	3,3	11		ger
(ex Yulence-87, London Miller-81)									
IBERIAN OCEAN (b)	79	1029	1391	72,2	11,3	3,3	11		ger
(ex Zealence-87, Birkenhead Miller-82)									
IBERIAN SEA (b)	88	1597	3366	85,1	13,0	6,0	11		ger
(launched as Ahmet Madenci II)									

Note. (b) - Bahamas flag

OWNERS/MANAGERS OF THE FOLLOWING VESSELS HAVE NOT BEEN FULLY IDENTIFIED

ISLAND MONARCH	57	419	690	51,1	9,0	3,4	9	gen
(ex Hunter-91, Arrow-89, Thoge-89, Partner-66)								

Note. Unregistered - laid up

PORT SOIF	71	426	645	47,8	8,8	3,1	8	gen
(ex Delce-90, Catrina Weston-84)								

Note. Flag ?

PIBROCH	57	151	160	26,5	6,1	2,9	9	gen

WILBERNIA	60	93	120	24,5	5,0	1,5	8	gen bge

ABBREVIATIONS FOR VESSEL TYPES

k tk	oil bunkering tanker
k tk bge	oil bunkering tank barge
ulk	bulk carrier
c(c)	container carrier (container capacity in Twenty foot Equivalent Units (TEUs))
em	bulk cement carrier
em bge	bulk cement barge
h tk	chemical tanker
ff tk	effluent tanker
sh	vivier tank fish carrier
en	general cargo
en(c)	general cargo (container capacity in TEUs)
en bge	general cargo barge
en/pt	general cargo/palletised cargo
og	liquified gas tanker
og(ch)	liquified gas tanker - chlorine
v	livestock carrier
uc	spent nuclear fuel carrier
il/bit tk	oil/bitumen tanker
il/ch tk	oil/chemical tanker
il/veg tk	oil/vegetable oil tanker
ef	refrigerated cargo
o	RoRo cargo
o(c)	RoRo cargo (container capacity in TEUs)
o/ch tk	RoRo cargo/chemical tanker
o/gen	RoRo cargo/general cargo
o h/l	RoRo heavy lift cargo
sand	sand and ballast carrier
sludge	sludge carrier
k	oil tanker
k bge	oil tank barge
k bge/gen	tank barge/general cargo
vt tk bge	water tank barge

KEY TO FLAGS

Antigua & Barbuda	(a)	Liberia	(l)
Bahamas	(b)	Malta	(m)
Cyprus	(c)	Norway (NIS)	(n)
Netherlands	(d)	Isle of Man	(o)
Vanuatu	(e)	Panama	(p)
Hong Kong	(f)	Poland	(q)
Gibraltar	(g)	Italy	(r)
Honduras	(h)	Germany	(s)
Irish Republic	(i)	Finland	(t)
St Vincent & the Grenadines	(j)	Luxembourg	(v)
Croatia	(k)	Denmark	(w)

.D.DISTRIBUTOR 45
;ABRIELE WEHR 42
;AMMAGAS 50
;ARDYLOO 37
;ARROCH HEAD 52
;AUSS F 48
;EM 51
;EORGE ODEY 13
;ERARD PATRICK PURCELL 49
;ERINA 54
;ERLENA 54
;ERLIN 54
;ERMAN 24
;ILBERT J. FOWLER 41
;INO 24
;LEN ... 26
;OODHAND 25
;ORDON THOMAS 10
;RACECHURCH X ... 24
;REEBA RIVER 39
;REENDALE H 17
;RETA C 9
;ROVEDALE 59
;RY MARITHA 30
;UIDESMAN 43

I. W. WILKINSON 45
1ARCUSS 53
1ARRIET 51
1ARTING 51
1AWESWATER 17
1ELEEN C 9
1ERNES 30
1EYO PRAHM 36
100 ... 30
100 X ... 30, 35
1OHEBANK 29
1OLM SOUND 24
1OPE 51
1ORNBURG 29
1OUND BANK 39
1OUNSLOW 13
1UELIN DISPATCH 28
1UMBER X ... 58, 59
1USNES 30

IBERIAN X ... 60
ILONA G 30
INISH ... 5
IRISHGATE 43
ISABEL 29
ISIS 4
ISLAND COMMODORE 11
ISLAND MONARCH 60
ISLAND SWALLOW 10

JAMES P 45
JAN BECKER 6
JAN KAHRS 6
JANA (1069/66) 4
JANA (3125/90) 6
JEVINGTON 51
JOHANNA 10
JOHN ADAMS 28
JOHN M 10
JOHNO 24
JONRIX 46

K/TOULSON 12
KAREN G 10
KATHE PRAHM 36
KELLS 22
KENMARE (2435/68) 14
KENMARE (5306/75) 23
KILLARNEY 22
KINDRENCE 12
KINGFISHER 52
KINSALE 23
KIRSTEN 10
KISH 3
KLAZINA C 9

LADY X ... 56
LANCING 51
LANCRESSE 20
LANRICK 26
LESZEK G 48
LIBATION 10
LOCATOR 45
LODELLA 45
LORD CITRINE 37
LORD HINTON 37
LORE PRAHM 36
LUBCHEM 51
LUMINENCE 12
LYRAWA BAY 6

MAERSK X ... 37, 38
MAGRIX 46
MALIN SEA 48
MARGARET G 10
MARK C 9
MARK PRIOR 45
MARPOL 12
MARTHA HAMMANN 36
MARY C 9
MATHILDE (3958/94) 15
MATHILDE (2363/71) 29
MATRISHA 8
MB X ... 3
MEDINA RIVER 41
MEDUNION 49
MERCATOR 14
MERCHANT X ... 56
MERKUR 15
MICHAEL ANE 41
MICHAEL M 10
MILLAC STAR II 8
MURIUS 59

NANCY 53
NATACHA C 9
NAUTIC W 25
NEPTUNUS 10
NEW GENERATION 22
NEWFYNE 3
NICHOLA G 10
NICHOLAS M 10
NOR ... 41
NORD STAR 41
NORDSTRAND 9
NORMAN COMMODORE 11
NORSKY 43
NORTH SEA TRADER 19

NORTHERN STAR 38
NORTHGATE 43
NORTHUMBRIA LASS 35
NUWAYBA 21

OARSMAN 43
ODERSTERN 46
ONWARD MARINER 4
OTTO BECKER 6

PALBRO PRIDE 14
PAMELA C 8
PAMELA EVERARD 19
PANARY 23
PEARL REEFER 39
PENTLAND 20
PERFECTO 12
PETER P 45
PETRO X ... 44, 45
PEVERIL 29
PHILIPP 29
PHILOMENA PURCELL 49
PIBROCH 60
PIQUENCE 12
PORT SOIF 60
PORTLAND 20
PUMA 44
PURBECK 11

OUENTIN 26
QUIESCENCE 12

RADNES 30
RAFNES 30
RAIDER 21
RAPID II 8
RATH ... 15
REBECCA HAMMANN 36
REDTHORN 11
REEDNESS 14
REMA 27
RISNES 30
RIVER DART 26
RIVER LUNE 38
RIVER TRADER 19
RIX X ... 46
ROAN 47
ROBERT M 11
ROBRIX 46
ROCK ... 16, 17
ROCQUAINE 17
ROFFEN 45
ROGUL 45
ROINA 40
ROMEO 3
RONEZ 50
ROSEANNE 14
ROSEBAY 14
ROSETHORN 11
ROSITA MARIA 6
ROUSTEL 8
RUDDERMAN 43
RUTLAND 53

SAFE HAND 37
SAFIYE SULTAN 54

63